Alexander Wylie

**Labour, Leisure and Luxury**

A Contribution to Present Practical-Political Economy

Alexander Wylie

**Labour, Leisure and Luxury**
*A Contribution to Present Practical-Political Economy*

ISBN/EAN: 9783744644914

Printed in Europe, USA, Canada, Australia, Japan

Cover: Foto ©Suzi / pixelio.de

More available books at **www.hansebooks.com**

# OPINIONS OF THE PRESS.

So much dangerous or sentimental rubbish is being talked to working men in these days, that it is a pleasure to come across a book like this.

The author is a friend of the working classes in the best sense.

He is an employer of labour who feels that he has other duties to perform to his hands besides paying them wages.

He speaks with the authority of experience, and also with sympathy.—*Saturday Review*.

Are not only a contribution to practical political economy, but furnish material for estimating the difference between the present and past condition of the labouring classes.

Its facts and teachings all go to prove that the drastic ideas of the levellers would in the end be fatal to true progress and subversive of the principles on which alone society can exist.

The author deals in an agreeable and informing manner with labour, leisure, luxury, progress, and the acquisition of property by the working classes; and the working classes cannot do better than study his simple chapters on political economy.—*Times*.

The facts he brings forward are important, thoroughly to the purpose, and are the results of close and long continued observation of the ways and conditions of working men; whilst the arguments deduced from them are sound and eminently practical.

The general tendency of his teaching is, that the future of the working class lies in their own hands; that, though much may be done, as, indeed, much has already been done, by wise legislation to ameliorate their condition, by far the largest share of the work can be effected by themselves alone.

To approach the status of the class immediately above them, they must acquire the qualities and virtues of that class. They must become more sober, more self-respecting, more provident, and more self-denying.

Till this transformation is effected all help from without is little better than thrown away.

In the chapter 'On the Acquisition of Property by the Working Classes' he enters into more definite details.

He sets before working-men, as the ultimate goal, co-operation.

For this, too, the moral qualities above named must be acquired.

He advises distributive co-operation, in the first instance, as intrinsically advantageous, but, still more, as the fittest school for the acquisition of those qualities and aptitudes which will enable them eventually to undertake with advantage productive co-operation, like that carried on by the Rochdale Pioneers, but which has so often failed in other cases from want of business habits and especially of self-control among the members.

It is true that in 1881 the number of co-operative societies had grown to 1,118, with 1,083,000 members, capital 6,850,000l., and sales equal to 24,400,000l. 'An enormous and most encouraging advance during twenty years,' says Mr. Wylie, 'nearly one-fourth of the working classes being now co-operators.

'The bulk of these societies, however, exist not for producing merchandise, but for selling it. . . . The want of success in productive co-operation is very easily accounted for.

'To conduct a manufacturing business properly requires a larger amount of intelligence than the mass of the working people possess.

'But their great want—a want shared by other classes as well—is in the morality necessary for the accumulation and guidance of sufficient capital, and, above all, to enable them to combine and act harmoniously together.'

He is no advocate of any further shortening of the working hours of adults, at any rate, for the present.

He shows that British workmen, while receiving higher wages than in any other country in Europe, work shorter hours than any other workmen in the World, America not excepted.

And he says, 'I have no hesitation in advising working men, and particularly trades unionists, to strive for the three following much more important advantages, before they seek further to reduce their hours of labour, viz., First: More leisure for their children—that is, to keep them longer out of the factory, and longer in school—in short, to let them begin life with better health and better education.

'Second: More leisure in the households, by keeping their wives and daughters more from factory work, and letting them attend more to the domestic duties, their natural sphere; and third, more leisure for themselves and families in time of sickness, and in the decline of life.'— *The Economist.*

He is entitled to speak with an authority that deserves to be listened to with more than ordinary respect.

His book is the result of wide observation and careful study, and is, pervaded from beginning to end with a wise, practical common sense which is of infinitely more value than the most brilliant speculations of the merely theoretical professor of what has not inaptly been called 'the dismal science.' It is one of those books, indeed, which deserves to be issued in a popular form, and to be read by all classes of society.

Mr. Wylie writes with great force and lucidity, and in our opinion has here furnished the solution to some of the most important problems of the day.—*The Scottish Review.*

Rightly described as dealing with Political Economy in its 'practical' form, not as a mere theory on paper.

He is a true friend of the working man and an optimist.

Altogether it is the most satisfactory book, of the kind, that we have met with.—*The Oxford University Herald.*

No more opportune time than the present could have been chosen for the publication of this book, and we trust the good, solid advice it contains will not be without its effect in agitating the thinking faculties of those social economists who are much too ready to favour the fantastic theories which seem to have acted on the masses like a beautiful optical illusion.

He commences his task with one clear and definite purpose before him, and, with all the force of which he is master, endeavours to plant it firmly and securely in the minds of his readers. His one thought which this book is written to lay down, amplify, and prove, is that any improvement in the condition of the working classes 'rests principally with themselves, and is mainly dependent upon their advancement in intelligence and morality.'

Never has the moral aspect of this great social problem been so strongly and effectively discussed before.

To our mind the chapter on 'Luxury' is the most interesting of the whole work. The subject is presented in a novel light, and it is so severely practical that it demands careful perusal and deep reflection.

Having gone carefully and connectedly through the details of his subject, the reader feels that he has traversed an unbroken chain of evidence leading him to an irresistible conclusion that there should 'be a more extended possession of property,' and that the first duty of the working man should be the acquisition of property.—*The Dumfries and Galloway Courier and Herald.*

The keynote of Mr. Wylie's advice to the industrial classes is, 'help yourselves.'. Mr. Henry George has recently been advocating legislation which would give a different meaning to this same piece of advice.

He would have the labourers ' help themselves ' to the property of their neighbours.  Mr. Wylie, however, shows up the fallacy of the communistic panacea, whereby the vicious and intemperate would be enabled to squander at the expense of the thrifty and industrious.

He advocates self-help as the chief means of amelioration.

If for no other reason, Mr. Wylie's pages would be valuable as counteracting the pretensions of those who profess to abolish the inequality of property, and all its attendant evils, by a single, simple legislative enactment, who vainly imagine that they can change human nature by Act of Parliament.

Mr. Wylie deserves our thanks for this opportune contribution to the practical political economy of the day.—*The Literary World.*

Brings prominently before the readers, not only the average income of the working classes, but the way in which it is spent.

This volume should be in the hands of every employer of labour and of every man who reflects a little on the sad position of many of his neighbours, especially at the present time of difficulty in finding occupation.

Mr. George proposes to give the land of England to the people ; we show the people a way of keeping the rent of land in their pockets instead of pouring it down their throats.—*British Trade Journal.*

Many well-meaning people start trying to improve the position of the working classes without having the slightest idea of the causes which bring about distress or the means which exist for elevating their social condition.

Mr. Wylie's collection of lectures on ' Labour, Leisure, Luxury ' will form a good handbook for such beginners.

If Mr. Wylie's book teaches a few people that statistics are not only useful but also interesting reading, he will have done good work.—*The Charity Organisation Review.*

Full of good advice to workmen and employers.—*The Graphic.*

There is some good-sense in Mr. Wylie's ' Contributions to Present Practical Political Economy,' and various statistical facts are presented in a forcible way, and with judicious comment.—*The Spectator.*

The teaching is sound and thorough, and is set forth with clearness and precision.

The author speaks out with characteristic Scotch plainness.—*Lloyd's Weekly London Newspaper.*

It is evident that he has carefully studied the present condition of our artisans, as well as the varied panaceas which have been put forth by leaders of their own class, and by others also.

Mr. Wylie looks at things from his own point of view.
Good sense and moderation prevail throughout. Mr. Wylie, while
in favour of many political reforms, would respect the rights of all
classes.—*The Nonconformist.*

Intelligent men might do far worse than follow the advice of
Mr. Wylie.—*The Inquirer.*

The appearance of this valuable book is certainly opportune.
It will meet with cordial assent to almost every proposition it
contains.
We ask our readers earnestly to get hold of this volume for them-
selves.
The paper is invaluable.—*The Social Reformer.*

We believe the book to be an honest and not unsuccessful attempt
to deal with certain social questions in such a way as to be at once
instructive and profitable to the working classes to whom these pages
are primarily addressed.
The book itself seems to us to be in two ways a sign of the times.
First, that a large employer of labour, such as Mr. Wylie apparently
is, should care to address his workpeople and neighbours on such topics
as those treated in this book, is itself a hopeful sign; and next, the
way in which, and point of view from which, the topics are handled,
are also characteristic.
One main purpose of the writer is to point out how questions of
political economy in every direction run up into, and are conditioned
by, questions of morality, and that it is impossible satisfactorily to treat
the former, while leaving the latter out of sight.
This is a point of view with which, in the main, we most cordially
concur.
The chapter on ' Luxury,' the third of these essays, seems to us the
most original and the most important chapter in the book.
Almost anyone might read it with entertainment and advantage.
An American economist has lately expressed a wish that there might
arise a new Adam Smith to write for our benefit a treatise on the
' Economics of Consumption.' Mr. Wylie has furnished us with at least
one serviceable chapter in this direction.
He has the root of the matter in him, and will prove in many ways
a safer guide than some more pretentious apostles.—*The Guardian.*

As resident partner in the great dyeing and printing works situate
in the busy village of Renton, near Dumbarton, where Tobias Smollett
first saw the light, and having in his employment a large percentage of
the 5,000 operatives who form its inhabitants, he has had exceptional

opportunities for studying their industrial and domestic life.—*The London Daily Telegraph.*

It is refreshing to come upon the remarks and opinions of a man who has a practical knowledge of the subject, and who never in all the cures he suggests loses sight of the fact that he is dealing, not with a machine that will act in strict conformity with mathematical rules, but with human nature and all its countless complications, uncertainties, and possibilities.

On another important point Mr. Wylie speaks with no uncertain sound, and that is the individual responsibility of each human creature for the making or the marring of his own well-being.

Mr. Wylie treats of labour, leisure, luxury, progress, and the acquisition of property by the working classes, and on all these heads he says wise and kindly things, and gives advice that deserves consideration because it comes from one who knows what he is talking about.—*The Glasgow Herald.*

Some masters are content to look upon their employés as so many 'machines' from which a certain amount of work is expected, but Mr. Wylie sees in them human beings endowed with passions like himself, whom force of circumstances has made hewers of wood and drawers of water.

He knows that the water must be drawn and the wood hewn, but he is determined that the yoke shall be as light and easy as possible, and that some sweetness and comfort shall be infused into the life of the labourer.

This is Mr. Wylie's creed, and in endeavouring to carry it into practice he has just published a treatise on 'Labour, Leisure, and Luxury,' a contribution to present practical political economy, worthy the closest attention of all sections of the community.

Such are the truths that Mr. Wylie has been seeking to inculcate among his own people for the last few years, and now that he appeals to a wider field we can only wish him 'God speed' in the good work.— *The North British Daily Mail.*

Mr. Wylie writes with a complete knowledge of his subject. He has no interest in making 'points,' indeed, he is too much in earnest to care about 'points.' All he says is said out of a full and anxious heart.

He has been brought into continual contact with a considerable section of the working and manufacturing classes of Scotland, and it is no more than justice to say that he has been induced to make a diligent study of their position and prospects from motives of genuine philanthropy.

We cannot believe that any intelligent working man will read Mr. Wylie's thoughtful pages without being forced to the conclusion that he is addressed in no selfish class-spirit, but that the writer has his best and truest well-being at heart.

Mr. Wylie is entirely practical.

He is not a dreamer of dreams like Mr. William Morris, or a social revolutionist like Mr. Henry George.

With both of these visionaries he thinks that there is a noble future for the artisan and wage-earning classes of this Kingdom. But he has no confidence in any millennium to be brought about, like the transformation-scene in a pantomime, by the wave of an enchanter's wand.

Amid the many wild and impracticable theories floating about, and never more audacious and menacing than at this particular juncture, it is refreshing to meet with a volume so replete with tranquil encouragement and wise and temperate counsel, set forth in kindly and eloquent words, and suffused with a spirit calculated to disarm jealousy and enmity.

Mr. Wylie is a capitalist and an employer of labour, but he has likewise shown himself to be, on disinterested grounds, a friend to the working man.—*The Glasgow Evening Citizen.*

It is always pleasant to find in the employer of labour a teacher of that wisdom which seeks to inspire the army of workers—first, to efforts of self-conquest, and then to the achievement of those economic victories which are the result of intelligent, patient, and honest industry, thrift, and temperance, from which spring the flower and fruitage of social virtue.

The book is not the production of the mere literary essayist, setting forth the results of his explorations through the well-packed shelves of his library.

Mr. Wylie is a practical man.—*The Glasgow Weekly Herald.*

The racy and popular form in which he has cast the earlier parts of this work render the rather deep subject of political economy highly interesting to the general reader.—*The Glasgow News.*

It is refreshing to receive so much common-sense as is embodied in this treatise, after the vast amount of Georgian vapouring recently presented on every hand.—*The Glasgow Evening News.*

A series of lectures and articles originally produced at different times, but carefully revised and brought up to the present date so far as their statistics are concerned.

. Mr. Wylie's economic principles are sound, and the advice he gives to working men is good and practical.—*The Scotsman*, Edinburgh.

This is a really important contribution to political economy. Working men can be strongly recommended to go and study it. They cannot have better advisers than Mr. Wylie.—*The Edinburgh Courant.*

The sooner the working classes learn that legislative socialism has no scientific support, and that the new gospel is contradicted alike by the laws of expediency and justice, the brighter will be the prospects of democracy.

As a protest against the new creed that men should be provided for according to their needs rather than their deserts, nothing could be more timely than the publication of a book entitled ' Labour, Leisure, and Luxury,' by Mr. Wylie, who has done good service as an economist. It is indeed a valuable contribution to economic science.

Its fundamental merit consists in bringing men's thoughts back to the old-fashioned doctrine, the soundness of which is admitted by the deepest sociological teaching of to-day, that national evil has its root in individual evil, and that the former can only be reached through the latter.—*The Edinburgh Evening News.*

The statistics they contain being brought up to 1884.

The author urges with much force and propriety the more scientific application of ' labour,' dwells with emphasis on the use and abuse of ' leisure,' and, while cheerfully admitting the material progress of the working classes during the last forty years, protests against the ' luxury ' and the enormous loss thereby sustained through excessive indulgence in intoxicating liquor.

He has a particularly interesting chapter on ' The Acquisition of Property by Working Men.'

The economic principles advocated throughout the volume are sound in every respect.

We cordially commend this book as essentially one for the present era of social reform.—*The Liverpool Mercury.*

The author is the resident partner of one of the largest and best-known Turkey-red dyeing and printing firms in Scotland—a firm, by-the-bye, which has been previously represented in literature.

Mr. Wylie has, however, followed one train of thought throughout the series.

He is one of those who believe that ' over-production ' should be converted into increased leisure and increased luxury for the producers.

To say this is to say that he earnestly desires to see wealth and poverty approximate; he does not believe that political economy has said its last word if it leaves us with the few very rich and the many abjectly poor.

This experience has led him to the conclusion that, although legislative enactment and outside philanthròpic effort may do much, the improvement of the economic condition of the working classes rests principally with themselves, and is mainly dependent upon their advancement in intelligence and, above all, morality.

It is worth while to point out that this is really the lesson which the English Trade Union delegates to the Labour Conference in Paris urged upon their revolutionary Continental brethren.

We hope Mr. Wylie's book will be widely read by capitalists, and still more widely by the working classes.

It is a good antidote to the rash utterances of a number of people who are just now doing some mischief by talking nonsense.—*The Manchester Guardian.*

The book is well worth reading by all who are interested in social reform.—*The Sheffield and Rotherham Independent.*

He is evidently in earnest.

The work will be found of real value to the student of political economy.

On the whole, Mr. Wylie's book may be regarded as a valuable contribution to modern Sociology.—*The Sheffield Daily Telegraph.*

The author is resident partner in a well-known firm—one of the largest employers of labour in Dumbartonshire—and has always taken a deep interest in the industrial and domestic life of the families under his charge. And he is no theorist. He has no quack nostrums to propound—no simple and sovereign panacea for poverty and crime.

He is thoroughly acquainted with his subject, and pre-eminently practical.

To improve, to elevate the economic conditions of the working classes is his great aim.

But it is by themselves mainly that this amelioration is to be effected—by the old-fashioned agencies of thrift and sobriety and self-denial—and not at once, by leaps and bounds, but gradually and by slow degrees.

It is a 'wholesome' and seasonable work. Well for the workman who makes it his manual of economics, and we heartily wish it a large circulation.—*The Dumbarton Herald.*

His book is the best antidote to the pernicious communistic theories which are so much in vogue in the present day. We trust that it will be widely read and studied by working men.—*Stirling Journal and Advertiser.*

We thoroughly recommend this little volume to the working man.—*The Perthshire Advertiser.*

The working classes, especially, would benefit from a perusal of his thoughtful papers. The work is one which we can commend to the notice, not only of the working people, but also of those who are striving to help them to help themselves.—*The Derby Mercury.*

Fine, thoughtful, well-informed, instructive, and suggestive essays.

His counsels, warnings, appeals, are well founded, and have a force, a directness of aim, a weight, which at once strike the thoughtful reader.

Mr. Wylie is the real friend of the working classes, though he does show that the amelioration of their position is mainly in their own hands.

Self-reform he shows to be at the basis of all true reform, and without this, Acts of Parliament will do, and can do little for us. This volume is as wise as it is comprehensive, and as solid as it is entertaining.

No political club ought to be without it, for it discusses in a calm, temperate, and honest spirit some of the most pressing and most important questions in practical political economy.

Working men will find the volume one of the most helpful that they have ever read.—*The Oldham Chronicle.*

Persons who desire to obtain an elementary knowledge of the results of labour and industry may study with advantage the three L's as here discussed, which are to workmen what the three R's are to scholars.—*The Inverness Courier.*

In its present form, we are afraid, this inestimable book will not find its way into the hands of the class Mr. Wylie is desirous of benefiting.

A cheaper edition is what some philanthropic individual should scatter over the country.

Is on a par with Smiles's 'Thrift,' and we trust 'Labour, Leisure, and Luxury' will have as large a sale as that work.

No mechanics' institute or reading-room should be without Mr. Wylie's book.—*Oban Times.*

Quite up to the level of the most recent thought and information. We can speak very highly of the real worth and permanent value of the book.

Talking patiently as if to an audience, and backing up every statement, when necessary, with statistics, the author really manages to impart a mass of most earnest thought and profitable counsel to his hearers.—*The Ayr Observer and Galloway Courier.*

We can cordially recommend Mr. Wylie's volume to the notice of working men, as it is a substantial contribution to practical political economy, a true understanding of which is so much needed at the present time.—*The Dundee Courier and Argus.*

An exceedingly able and suggestive work.

Certainly no social reformer, or person who desires to understand the failings and needs of the working classes, should fail carefully to study this valuable contribution to modern sociology.—*Lincoln, Boston, and Spalding Free Press.*

Mr. Wylie is obviously gifted with literary talent very far beyond the average, combined with a power of observation and a faculty of logic which result in the production of matter at once polished and convincing.—*The Nottingham Daily Guardian.*

'He does not seek' to dive deeply into the past nor far into the future, but to define as exactly as possible the political economy of the present, to measure as nearly as need be the elevation to which our working classes have already attained, as compared with their immediate past, and to point out to themselves, and all interested in their welfare, their next steps still further upwards.

This volume may be said to be a full armoury of thoughts and facts for the writer and the lecturer.—*The Warrington Guardian.*

The book is interesting, instructive, and valuable.

We can do no more than heartily commend the volume to our readers, especially those of the working classes.—*The Leicester Chronicle and Leicestershire Mercury.*

It is a work with the tenets of which we entirely agree.

No Government can do for the people what they can do for themselves.

The task of self-reform is well within the reach of all, and Mr. Wylie, following in the steps of William Cobbett and Samuel Smiles, points out how it may be done.

We hope the book will have a large circulation.—*The Mining World and Engineering Record.*

The questions indicated in the title are treated of in an interesting style, very different from the ordinary run of works on this subject, and a working man desirous of acquainting himself with the principles of political economy could not obtain a better book for the purpose than the one before us.—*The Bradford Daily Telegraph.*

A healthy remedy for the false and dangerous teaching that the advancement of the working classes in the social scale is to be effected by legislation, or at least by operations conducted from without.

A sound adviser and safe guide to the class which he addresses.

The book is well worth perusal, and if its advice were taken and its principles adopted by the working classes, the millennium would approach within measurable distance of at least that class of society.—*The Colliery Guardian.*

A welcome contribution to present practical political economy, and ought to be widely circulated amongst, and studied by, the classes for whose enlightenment it was written.—*The Bristol Mercury and Daily Post.*

An earnest tone underlies the whole, and the writer speaks with the authority of one who has studied his subject thoroughly, and who has besides dealt practically with the problems of labour and wealth.—*The Aberdeen Daily Free Press.*

His contributions to political economy have been well received, and we heartily recommend the present volume.

It is full of sound practical common sense, and is worthy of the most careful perusal.

The arguments are irresistible, the facts and figures being conclusive, and in this noble work we wish him every success.—*The Helensburgh and Gareloch Times.*

It is permissible to hope that he may live to see ripening under his eyes the golden harvest of his teaching.—*The Glasgow Evening Times.*

Those who have no sympathy with the pernicious doctrines of Socialism and Communism, will welcome this contribution to present practical political economy.

The writer is practical, and if his suggestions were adopted, they would conduce to the well-being of the whole community.—*The Halifax Guardian.*

# LABOUR, LEISURE

### AND

# LUXURY

### A CONTRIBUTION TO PRESENT PRACTICAL
### POLITICAL ECONOMY

BY

## ALEX. WYLIE

*of Glasgow*

---

'My heart rejoiced in all my Labour; and this was my portion
of all my Labour'—*Eccles.*

'And add to these retired Leisure,
    That in trim gardens takes his pleasure'—MILTON

'Luxury is indeed possible in the future—innocent and exqui-
site Luxury for all, and by the help of all'—RUSKIN

---

*NEW EDITION*

LONDON

## LONGMANS, GREEN, AND CO.

1887

PRINTED BY
SPOTTISWOODE AND CO., NEW-STREET SQUARE
LONDON

DEDICATED

TO THE MEMORY OF ONE

WHO STROVE TO IMPROVE THE CONDITION OF

THE WORKING CLASSES

AND MADE THE POOR HER CARE

M860994

# PREFACE TO POPULAR EDITION.

THE teaching of the most erroneous and subversive doctrines regarding property has been increasing and bearing fruit to an alarming extent.

If the need was great for the dissemination of sound views regarding the various problems of our complicated political economy in 1884, when this treatise was first published, it is even more so now.

A popular edition of 'Labour, Leisure, and Luxury' was from the first contemplated, as the treatise was written principally for the benefit of the working classes.

The author has all the more confidence and pleasure in putting such an edition into their hands seeing that this contribution to 'Present Practical Political Economy' has been so universally approved and commended by the Metropolitan and Provincial Press, and the issue of a cheap edition to bring it within the scope of workmen's income has been so strongly urged.

The issue of this edition has been taken advantage of to bring all the statistics as nearly as possible up to date, and thus place in the hands of our operatives a concise compendium of information regarding all the important items of our present political economy, selected from sources beyond their means and with practical suggestions carefully deduced from them.

As it deals largely with the extraordinary social and economic progress of the subjects of our gracious Sovereign Queen Victoria during the fifty years of her beneficent reign, it is the source of much congratulation to the Author that it is being issued in popular form in her Jubilee year, and of earnest hope that it may contribute in some small degree to still further increase the loyalty, prosperity, and amicable relationships of all classes in her dominions.

CORDALE, RENTON: *February* 1887.

# PREFACE.

IT has never been sought more strongly than at present to impregnate the minds of our working classes with the idea that the improvement of their condition is to be effected by means apart from themselves. I have therefore deemed this a fit time to publish in one treatise several articles written at different times, the main purport of which is to show that, whatever aid may be derived from legislative enactment or outside philanthropic effort (and I admit that there may be much), the improvement of their economic condition rests principally with themselves, and is mainly dependent upon their advancement in intelligence and, above all, morality.

No one would view with more satisfaction than myself the realisation of the sanguine theories of many social reformers who write of the glorious future of the working classes, but a long and practical acquaintance with the subject has more and more convinced me that their elevation, like everything else that is good and lasting, must be by slow degrees, and by the permeating influences of education and religion. Intelligence and morality shape the political economy of a people more than the material and physical conditions which surround them, and its form is ever varying. Our present political economy is very different from that of the Ashantees or Patagonians—very different even from our own of fifty years ago. This treatise does not seek to dive deeply into the past nor soar far into the future, but to define as exactly as possible the political economy of the present, to measure as nearly as need be the elevation to which our working classes have already attained as compared with their immediate past, and to point out to themselves and all interested in their welfare their next steps still further upwards.

Amongst them, I am happy to know, are thousands unsurpassed for intelligence and morals by any in the land, and

capable of taking their place in industrial associations far
ahead of their times, but they are 'bound in the bundle of life'
with immensely greater numbers who are now, and will be for
many years to come, incapable of united action by themselves,
and requiring the strong guidance of the capitalist, or, to use
the good old-fashioned word, 'the master.'

It is all very well to theorise and plan about things as they
should be, but we must first recognise existing conditions, and
then strive to better them in the full light of this knowledge.

This contribution to the political economy of the day—the
result, as I have said, of an intimate practical acquaintance
with the subject—will, I hope, help in some small degree to
dispel those communistic ideas, so prevalent in neighbouring
countries, from the minds of our working classes, and incite
them and their friends to renewed efforts for a better national
life in no revolutionary or theoretical, but in a thoroughly
conservative and practical spirit.

The chapter on 'Labour' appeared in 'Meliora, a quarterly
review of social science, a good many years ago, and formed a
small contribution to the public opinion which has found expression in the extension of factory legislation and the early
closing movements ; that on 'Luxury' in 'Fraser's Magazine'
for October 1872.

The chapter on 'Leisure' was delivered as a lecture at the
inauguration of the Renton Literary Society in 1881 ; that on
'Progress' at the inauguration of the Renton Mechanics' Institution in 1882 ; and that 'On the Acquisition of Property by
the Working Classes' as a lecture in the ordinary course of
said Institute in 1883.

Renton, of classical memory, as the birthplace of Tobias
Smollett, is a village of about 5,000 inhabitants, some of whom
find employment in the ship-building yards of the neighbouring town of Dumbarton, but the great majority in the Turkey-
red dyeing and printing works belonging to the firm of which
the writer is the resident partner, who has thus had special
facilities, greater than in a larger and more widely scattered
community, for studying intimately the industrial and domestic
life of a mixed manufacturing population, about two-fifths of
whom are Irish.

The treatise is specially concerning the manufacturing
classes, who now form the great majority of our workers, but
the general principles enunciated are applicable to all.

# CONTENTS.

——◆◆◆◆——

# CHAPTER I.

## LABOUR.

'ALL things are full of labour; man cannot utter it : the eye is not satisfied with seeing, nor the ear filled with hearing.'[1] Worlds wheel around worlds in endless course. The earth, a globular atom in the circling universe, rolls on, content not to be merely coalescing with the common mass, but maintaining its individuality by energetic rotation, and bearing on and within it multitudinous forms of action—its inorganic formations, with their inexpressibly gradual upheaval or subsidence ; its organic forms rising and decaying with unvaried constancy ; its atmosphere bearing to the appointed place the rain torrent ; its rivers rushing to their goals ; its mighty ocean resisting not the unseen influences, the tidal flow and ebb, currents and counter-currents, evidencing its subjection to the great and universal law ; the myriads of its animated forms moving restlessly over its surface, and presenting scenes of unceasing activity ; and the din of human toil, mingling with all nature's various sounds, with the roar of the cataract, the torrent's rush, the murmuring of many streams, the voices of breeze and storm over all lands, the dash of waters on every coast, the deep music of the lone ocean, and the varied sounds of bird and beast in the wilderness and the solitary place, ascends, a low and never-ceasing hum, to the arch of heaven continually.

'Thou shalt labour.' is the law of man's life. Ceaselessly, resistlessly, like the great power which works out the stupendous circle of all inanimate labour, operates the mighty principle of human impulsion. Inexorable, it acts through life, and will act throughout eternity. In spite of himself man must labour ; if he would he cannot rest. Like a planet, he has been launched into existence, possessing a power which he himself cannot annihilate ; which, if regulated aright, will

[1] Eccles. i. 8.

D

make him part of the grand, harmonious, concentric system ;
if not, will hurry him off at an abrupt tangent till he dash
himself to destruction.  Like the power of gravitation, drawing down the swollen volume of a great river's waters, or
impelling the majestic march of the ocean's tides, this force
may for a time be partially resisted ; but, ever gathering
larger weight, it either tosses all obstruction out of its natural
course, or, sweeping away its impotent object in another direction, involves all in dire ruin, in confusion worse confounded.
A mighty and wonderful agent in the hands of the Great
Worker has been this principle of human energy, acting in
the hundreds of generations which have passed as shadows
over earth's surface.  Although in the great arena of universal
labour it has lifted, as it were, but a grain of sand in helping
to work out one of the stupendous plans of the Omnipotent,
yet in the sphere of this world's work it has done much.  It
has become one of the most potent and active of earthly
agencies.  The last to be introduced, at first isolated and
insignificant, it has increased with the increase of the human
race, and now forms the complement of the forces carrying
out the great cosmical operations ; and, dominating and con-
trolling many of the others, it has now assumed its rightful
position as chief.  By its agency, in part, the glorious amelioration of the material, which shall accompany the advancement
of the spiritual, world in 'the latter days' is fast progressing.

But the good God, who has appointed to everything, ani-
mate and inanimate, its full share of labour, surely intended
that in the performance of it all His living, and especially His
intelligent creatures, should find their *enjoyment*.  Labour has
this 'profit,' and a valuable one it is, in itself.  In almost all
countries, under almost all climates, we find men thoroughly
appreciating it for this, its first, reward ; with enough of satisfaction in working for their 'mere good pleasure' to induce to
active, continued exertion.

It would have been as easy for the 'All Giver' to have
provided for us all necessaries, comforts, and luxuries directly,
as indirectly, through the instrumentality of our own labours,
and to have removed from us all instant compulsion to exertion by advancing the operations of nature a single step
farther.  To fallen man this would have been a curse more
bitter than that by the sweat of his brow he must earn his
bread.  God has wisely given those things as the reward of, and
inducement to, that which is itself necessary ; has wisely given

the objects and furnished the immediate necessity for the
exercise of our physical and mental powers. Only a very
slight further modification of our surroundings would have been
sufficient to have annihilated the many inexorable physical
necessities which now summon us to a life of labour ; but inasmuch as the whole material world has been left just in such
a nicely-balanced condition as to demand for its utilisation
the healthy exercise, and no more, of all our faculties, it is
evident that in the Creator's design the grand object of all
labour is the improvement of the labourer. By its own labour
everything tends to the perfection of its kind. Besides the simple
pleasure in work, for which alone it is often undertaken, and
the material value which productive labour creates, our faculties are silently but surely taking to themselves from every
action which they perform aright that which is superior to
both. When work is finished, when its tangible produce is
consumed, and the evanescent joy in the performance of it has
vanished, more lasting results still remain with the labourer—
more power and superior skill (which is aptitude for perform-
ing again the same work more easily and successfully) remain
with the members of the body which have been exercised ;
keener intellect from the exercise of the mental faculties ;
superior morality with the striving soul. Labour, under whatever name known, is the only means of human improvement.

Idleness or sloth, the attempt—and it can be no more than
an attempt—to evade the universal law of labour, is only a
short pause, during which all that is good in humanity is rot-
ting, and evil powers are germinating which will soon spring
up and urge to fearful activity ; just as the same water which,
when flowing along in its river course, an emblem of the beautiful and joyously free, cherishes the noble vegetation of trees
and flowers, confers upon its country health and wealth, and
bears the gallant ships that pass thereby ; when stagnating in
the level marsh seems at first quiescent, then fosters every
dank and putrid thing, and spreads unwholesome malarious
vapours over earth's surface. Sloth is a part of that sinister
bent which pervades the whole character of fallen man, and
impels him to act contrary to the laws of his nature. We
must admire the goodness which did not leave it at our own
option, but forced upon us by the stern compulsion of physical
wants to act in accordance with this great law of our being;
to comply naturally and easily with the inexorable necessity, to taste the pleasure which the exercise of our faculties

confers, to apply this only means for our improvement; and our working classes, who are so immediately and peremptorily under this compulsion, should ponder well the advantages which it secures to them.

All that has been said of the benefits of labour refers to it when temperate and well directed. If there is decreed unto us the inexorable law of labour, most ample provision has been made by our Creator, the whole economy of nature has been adapted to secure to us seasonable rest. Compound man, possessed of many faculties, each and all ready for use, requiring for the formation of the complete man that they shall be used, is not exhausted with the exhaustion of any one of his divers powers, but is prepared, and even disposed, to exercise the others, and is thus beneficently furnished with *recreation*—the pleasant, grateful rest of his tired, but not over-fatigued, with the active, delightful employment of his fresh faculties. To it we hope all work shall become more and more assimilated.

The wise man tells us that 'There is nothing better for a man than that he should eat and drink, and make his soul enjoy good in his labour.'[1] 'Happiness is health.' And not on the workman only, but likewise on his work, does his delight in it act beneficially. It may be laid down as a rule that the highest excellence in any work, whether mental or physical, can only be attained by aid of the workman's pleasure in it. Of mind and body, the best and strongest, most vigorous and graceful, efforts are put forth, not under the pressure of overwhelming and harassing tasks, but as the spontaneous, exultant efforts of a system attuned by the ease of nerve and muscle springy and elastic with the latent power, eager for use, stored up in them by rest; of a system permeated with the feeling of joy, or at least calm satisfaction, in exerting itself.

But *intemperate labour* destroys all the delight which a man should find in his work; instead of improving the faculties exercised by it, it grinds them down, impairs, and prematurely destroys them; instead of giving health and strength, and making bone and sinew active and skilful, instead of developing the mental powers, instead of quickening and exalting the virtues and graces of the soul, it strongly helps to make the body stunted, diseased, and deformed—to superinduce a sleepless, raving insanity, or, by softening and enfeebling the brain,

---

[1] Eccles. ii. 24.

imbecility and idiocy. It deadens and corrupts the soul. God only knows how much of refinement and love, how much of all that most truly ennobles man, has been, 'as with an iron nerve, put down;' how much of wit and knowledge and ingenuity and genius annihilated, or altogether subverted; how much of athletic vigour and superb gracefulness changed into feeble deformity by over-exertion; how much of comfort and happiness swept as by an avenging angel from the lot of poor humanity; how many of those good things for which itself was undertaken wasted and lost; how many persons hurried to premature graves; how many more obliged to toil on through their dreary lives without a glimpse of that joy which awaited only the bidding of relaxation to rush in like a flood; how many, endowed with splendid mental powers, have found their light of reason overclouded or wasted down into drivelling idiocy; how many poor toiling wretches have had all their virtue and all their hope crushed out by this, in many cases self-imposed, evil. We are often told—it is one of the practices of our day to write and lecture—of men whose ambitious souls fix upon some great aim, impossible of realisation to ordinary wills—dazzling, glorious—the attainment of which, ever before their mind's eye, becomes the one object of their lives; adamantine resolve to succeed, the spring of all their action. We are told that by years of toil, toil from which common mortals would shrink, toil hard, unrelaxing, despotic, they do succeed; but it is seldom revealed to us, it seldom can be revealed, at what heavy, heavy cost the prize has, in many instances, been purchased. The unthinking multitude, who see the outward halo of triumph around the heroes' heads, clap hands, and shout, 'Well done! well done!' The ambitious, toiling far down on that same ladder which has led up to fame and fortune, look up and see them exalted, as they think, near the heavens, among the gods. They take example and encouragement, and seek to imitate by fierce effort. Many who take upon themselves to show to youth the way of 'success in life' point up to where they sit, their labour done, and bid their pupils emulate. The successful themselves often think that they have triumphed gloriously. But if some divine power would raise up in their minds' chamber of imagery the glowing picture of what their lives would have been if moulded by the influence of temperate, though earnest, labour, contrasting it side by side, step by step, character produced by character produced, with what their lives have

been, the steel-nerved men would weep at the contrast, and
execrate the poor, worthless shadow of which they have possessed themselves. And if the multitude who cite them as
examples, and the fewer who make of them their pattern,
could see how many sink to rise no more in their intemperate
efforts; how many toil on without success, their too great
eagerness marring the very ends at which it aims; how many
subvert what would otherwise have been noble lives—public
opinion and practice would be greatly modified. 'Our Creator,'
says Dr. Southwood Smith, 'has given us a frame capable of
a certain degree of labour—capable of putting forth a certain
degree of energy and no more. If we disregard the limits
which He has put to our capability of exertion, that beautiful
and delicate mechanism, upon the action of which our life
depends, must be deranged—must break.' Dr. James Copland
states :—'There is nothing which can be more injurious, both
mentally and physically, to the middle and lower classes of
society than prolonged labour. I believe that three-fourths of
the disease to which human life is liable in the metropolis
actually arises from this cause.' R. D. Grainger, Esq., gives
the following testimony :—'I would say, without fear of con-
tradiction from any quarter worthy of attention, I would
pledge all I know of the constitution of the human frame to
the assertion, that protracted labour is nothing else than
another term for sickness, suffering, and death. There is no
exception to this rule.' And mark that overwork tells upon
the growing child, whose bone is but gristle, in a tenfold
degree. In many employments not under Government supervision the overwork of British children is still an evil to be
strongly deplored.

The overwork of children in school is just now occupying
a great deal of attention in England,[1] though I am not aware
that there is much complaint in Scotland. But the proper
temperate exercise of the faculties during the period of childhood is a matter of supreme importance for the whole of their
after life, and the physiology of each individual child should
be carefully studied, so that no harassing tasks, either physical
or mental, should be imposed upon him. Dr. Lankester, of
London, says :—'I find that there is in this metropolis a
sacrifice of a thousand lives annually through the practice of
keeping shops open for a greater number of hours than the

[1] See Note 1 in Appendix to 'Labour.'

human constitution can bear. But this is not all. Where a thousand persons die annually from this cause, there are at least eight thousand whose health suffers from it.' In this, as in many other forms of employment throughout the country, the more delicate and sensitive strength of the woman is largely overtaxed.[1] A great many of our tradesmen and other male labourers, such as bakers, tailors, shoemakers, 'bus drivers, &c., are also still being subjected to too prolonged and unhealthy over-exertion. Many railway accidents have resulted from the extremely prolonged hours to which the servants of the railway companies have been exposed. In one case a company was prosecuted for overworking a poor 'engine-cleaner who was burned to death in an engine in which he had fallen asleep through exhaustion, after working thirty-six hours without relief.' In another case, where an engine-driver and brakesman were apprehended and fined 10l. for being drunk on duty, 'one of the prisoners stated that he had been on duty for nineteen hours at a stretch.' Evidence on this point is not scanty. Similar examples could be extracted from hundreds of sanitary pamphlets and reports. Almost the whole of these have reference, not to pure mental, but to mixed bodily and mental, or altogether manual, labours ; but it is well known that all intellectual operations are carried on by aid of physical organs, the brain being the grand instrument of thought, and that this organism is, in a greater degree even than that which enables us to prosecute muscular toil, subject to exhaustion. Intense intellectual is certainly more exhaustive than the most severe physical exertion; and of the two forms of intemperate work—mental and manual—the former is decidedly the more injurious. Its baneful effects are found in the impaired digestion, general physical debility, relaxed will, and (in extreme cases) the softened brain, clouded reason, idiocy, or madness of its devotees. It is well that at the present time so much observation is being bestowed upon these its results by many of the literary and scientific, and that, owing to the melancholy fate of several giant workmen of the mind, directly traceable to this cause, the subject is receiving universal attention. I was speaking to one of the leading clergymen of Glasgow the other day on this subject, and he was bewailing the frequent prostration from nervous exhaustion, and premature death, caused by too much brain-work amongst his clerical

[1] See Note 2 in Appendix to 'Labour.'

brethren, especially the young ministers, who were now far
sooner than formerly thrust into or thrust themselves into
city charges.

It is a common fallacy of our age and race, if not openly
avowed, at least largely acted upon, to suppose that it is
impossible to labour too much. Intemperate labour is one of
the most prominent and peculiar characteristics of the Anglo-
Saxon. His manly, independent, active temperament, which
has mainly contributed to give him his predominating influence
in the family of nations, has, to a great extent, impelled him
to an excess of industry, injurious and vicious. The position
of prime importance which labour, mental as well as physical,
occupies in the social structure, and the powerful and essential
influences which it exerts on national prosperity, were never
before so thoroughly understood and appreciated. The upper
classes, more enlightened and refined than their ancestors, now
cordially acknowledge the advantages and dignity of labour ;
and many of them, by precept, influence, and example, are
urging on and directing the industrial community in its own
special pursuits. None are more zealous in diffusing and
popularising the maxims inculcating diligence and perseverance
than many of our modern authors, themselves too often setting
the example of over-straining toil. Cases are not rare in
which men of letters wear down their brains to soft pulp in a
few years. Many of our merchants and manufacturers themselves, in their too great haste to be rich, set an example of
restless activity, dragging their employés up to a similar pitch
of exertion. But, of a truth, the workmen, in most instances,
need little spurring or dragging. Their own active temperament, and the love of the greater gains which 'overtime'
procures, make them willing coadjutors in the system of long
hours. Perhaps, without exception, the Anglo-Saxon workman, whether handicraft, manufacturing, mercantile, professional, or literary, is the hardest wrought in the world. The
tide of over-labour which has swept over this country with
desolating effects (wherein the sufferings of the over-wrought
children are perhaps most to be deplored), and which, strange
to say, has received vast impetus from the introduction of our
new machinery and important discoveries in the physical
sciences, probably reached its highest mark before the year
1833, when the Factory Act, regulating the hours of work
for women and children, was passed ; and although since that
time there has been improvement, yet there is still urgent

need for the prosecution of the nation's work in methods more in accordance with the laws of human physiology. 'The great cry that rises from all our manufacturing cities, louder than their furnace blast, is all in very deed for this, that we manufacture everything there except men.' The Lancashire operative, dwarfed in height, thin, pale, narrow-chested, spindle-shanked, and on the average not living out half his days, was the type of a man produced by the system of labour, in the formation of which his own greed has borne an active share, and which, having seized upon him when a mere infant, kept him working on, with only forced pauses of relaxation, machinery's well-paid slave, whose best friends were glad to see him subjected to the compulsory short time, knowing that only thus would the pale face get a little brighter, the bent form a little straighter, the poor fellow, whose noble endurance of privation during the 'Cotton Famine' excited the admiration of the nation, a little more like a man; that only thus would his wife find time to attend to her natural duty instead of to the machine, and his children, though worse fed and more scantily clad, yet under a mother's care, and allowed to breathe more of the fresh air, and to bathe more in the healthful sunlight, should not so much swell those terrible tables of infantile mortality.[1]

It is undoubtedly splendid physical material which was, and in many cases is still, being thus deteriorated. The British and Americans are certainly the best of any workmen. Slave labour would be deemed mild exercise, and most of the free labour of other countries would be regarded as mere apprentice work by our stalwart working men. The negro on the cotton plantations of the Southern States is quite a deli-cate employé compared with the sturdy white labourer from Ireland ; and for the negro, during the time of slavery, were reserved the lighter tasks of hoeing, picking, planting, and other like operations, connected with the culture of cotton, in preference to the more laborious work of draining, embanking, &c., on which the aristocratic planter employed the more robust Irishman, who had in all likelihood served his apprenticeship to the turf-cutting trade, at the construction of some British railway, canal, or other engineering work, and could bear testi-

[1] It was a notorious fact, borne out by the then state of affairs in Lancashire, that a stoppage of the mills, though entailing a reduction of food, fuel, and clothing, was invariably attended by a decreased registration of deaths, especially of infants' deaths,

mony that the Scot and Englishman, who then wrought on each side of him, were quite as strong and expert with spade and pickaxe as himself. Mr. Edwin Chadwick, at the Social Science Congress held in Glasgow in 1860, said :—' I have been in a position to obtain the impartial testimony of foreign employers to the superior efficiency of the British labourers—that two British labourers do as much work as three modern Norwegians, or three modern Normans, or three modern Danes. Our sanitary engineer, Mr. Rawlinson, who directed works in the Crimea, avers that it would have been economical to have exported British labourers at five shillings a day to have performed the work done by the Easterns at less than one-fifth that rate of wages ; and British engineers who have conducted works in other parts of the world give similar testimony. The qualities which take the lead in mining and tunnelling take the lead in penetrating forests and clearances for colonisation. Volney and other French witnesses acknowledge the superiority of the Anglo-Saxon in this respect.'

The report of the Royal Commission on Technical Instruction gives several striking instances of the superiority of British workmen.

'One large employer in Ghent thought that " good English workmen could do 20 per cent. more work in the same time than either Frenchmen or Germans. The English are more energetic and keep up the pace better. They have greater strength than their Continental rivals." Besides this, "mechanical industries in England are usually more concentrated, and English workmen have been brought up on a more liberal allowance of animal food than any on the Continent." '

The great and crushing drawback to the efficiency of the British workman is his intemperance,[1] to which I will refer at length when I come to treat of 'luxury.' His innate superiority as a worker, when he gives himself fair play, is, however, undoubted, and this superiority has been immensely supplemented. To us has been delegated a portion of the mighty power which has upheaved the everlasting hills, the awful nature of whose operations Etna, Chimborazo, and more than two hundred other burning mountains, still manifest to the appalled eye, giving it a glimpse of that which, though now by the beneficent will of its Author confined deep in the vaulted recesses of the earth, was at an earlier period of time in a state

[1] See Notes 3 and 4 in Appendix to 'Labour.'

of fiercest activity on its surface, and was then employed to open, as with a colossal wedge, some of those deep, extensive valleys which, now covered with vegetation, form the sheltered retreats of the sons of men. The Creator has made over to us, by means of the master-intellect of one or two of His more highly endowed creatures (for every time the rude and ignorant stoker grasps the iron handle by which he unchains the snorting monster, the mighty presiding genius of Watt and Stephenson stands, as it were, by his side, guiding and assisting the more untutored intellect to use aright the giant strength), the control of one of His own most powerful and important material agencies, heat, perhaps the mightiest and most active of that array of stupendous forces by which He carries on the world's work. This terribly energetic agency has been stored up in stupendous quantity in the immense coal-fields of the world, of which

|  | Square miles |
| --- | --- |
| Great Britain possesses . . . . . | 9,000 |
| France . . . . . . . . | 1,800 |
| Germany . . . . . . . . | 3,600 |
| Russia . . . . . . . . | 27,000 |
| Belgium, Spain, &c. . . . . . . . | 1,400 |
| Europe . . . . . . . . | 42,800 |
| United States . . . . . . . | 194,000 |
| India . . . . . . . . . | 35,000 |
| China . . . . . . . . . | 200,000 |
| Total . . | 471,800 |

The Parliamentary report shows that Great Britain possesses a coal supply of 90,000 millions of tons, enough for 600 years at our present rate of production, without going deeper than 4,000 feet.—(Mulhall's 'Dictionary of Statistics.')

Professor Rogers estimates that 'Each acre of a seam yielding three feet of pure fuel is equal to about 5,000 tons, and possesses a reserve of mechanical strength equal to the labour of 1,600 men during their whole life ; and each square mile of the same bed contains 8,600,000 tons of fuel, which is equal to one million of men labouring through twenty years of their ripe strength. The mass of coal in all the coal-producing districts of Europe and North America contains a latent force little inferior to that which could be used, during their whole lives, by sixteen milliards of men of average strength.' By means of 'the great wonder and wonder-worker of the age ; the greatest mechanical wonder perhaps of all ages that have been since the world began—the steam-engine,' this gigantic latent force becomes obediently, tirelessly, active in man's service. The total steam-power of the world is estimated as being equal to that of 28,952,000 horses, of which Great Britain alone has about 27 per cent., being 220 horses-power to every 1,000 inhabitants; whilst Belgium, the European country which comes next to us in manufacturing facilities, has 110, being only the half. *There has thus been acquired in this country an aid to labour equal to rather more than one horse-power to each family in it.* There never was in all the world's past life, there is not amongst its present numerous nations, as large a number of the human race united by bonds so strong and many as the population of Great Britain˙; nor such an example of systematised, combined labour as they display.

The immense difference between the industrial power of nations appears in the fact that the united labour of 6 British is equal to that of 24 French or Germans, 32 Austrians, 50 Spaniards, 75 Italians, or 84 Portuguese.[1]

No people has been more ingenious in the inventing and handling of those tools and machines which enable most easily to subdue the material world, nor have any employed to so large an extent the power of this new agency. It has become our universal slave. It ploughs the ground, cuts the crop, thrashes, grinds, and even bakes ; it spins the yarn, weaves the cloth, bleaches, prints, and finishes it ; to its other business has been added that of ocean-carrier ; finally, it makes its own harness by beating out the iron and turning the shafts required in the construction of steam machinery. Aided by the electric telegraph, it has already shown itself to be one of the most potent physical causes in linking into union yet more united the homogeneous elements of the nation, riveting by its iron rails, interweaving by its river, lake, and sea-going traffic, the separated yet nicely fitting parts into one more compact, firm-knit whole, yea, even stretching out and as with giant sweep bringing all mankind into a mighty commonwealth.

Thus skilled, thus knit into so intimate combination, possessing superior physical energy, and the vast power which a gigantic, systematised, united labour confers, and aided by this superb force, made so deftly applicable to almost every purpose by the instrumentality of the steam-engine, that grand tool

---

[1] Mulhall's *History of Prices*, p. 54.

placed in the hands of our highly developed civilisation, which requires not so much the exercise of sheer physical strength as the calm, active, patient, and intelligent supervision so well fitted to be the work of rational man, to what ends have we directed our most extended dominion over the material world ? The strength of the whole scientific machinery of this country is not less than that of one hundred millions of men ; and of that we have suddenly, easily, and economically obtained an acquisition of power equal to the united strength of seventy millions. Might not this acquisition, in many respects, be more wisely and beneficially applied than it has been? In no other way would it do more good than by being allowed to fulfil its primary, natural duty of alleviating and abridging the labours of the overworked portion of the industrial community. Many of the British workmen, at the period of the extensive introduction of steam machinery, who had not time to give the subject any consideration till it advanced in gigantic importance so near as to be seen from but one point of view, could perceive only the most prominent of its probable results magnified by the apprehension of injury to themselves, and were led to predict the almost total superseding of human labour ; and there was no lack of better educated, and even thoroughly clever men, who, calculating its future influence from the same narrow data, did not hesitate to espouse this idea, and to advance boldly a principle which, if acted upon to the extreme, would have abolished the use of implements altogether. ' Whenever the uses of our scientific machinery in abridging labour are explained to an intelligent Chinese, the first idea that strikes him is the disastrous effect that such a system would work upon his over-peopled country if suddenly introduced into it ; and he never fails to deprecate such an introduction as the most calamitous of visitations.' But one of the primary effects of the introduction of steam machinery has been, not to supersede, but, aided by other causes, in many cases to increase human labour, to incite to insane competition between human bone and muscle and the stalwart labourer of the iron limbs, and to foster a system of overwork which has been most prejudicial. Modern civilisation has been so proud of her newly invented and best material tool, so elated with its wonderful results and charmed by the ease and dexterity with which she can wield it, that in the first flush of success, flourishing it in her powerful grasp, she has overwrought and racked herself. The use of machinery is equivalent to the more beneficent gifts of nature—such as more fertile soil and genial climate—inasmuch as by it man is enabled to provide necessaries and comforts by a less expenditure of labour— with this difference, that these gifts, having no dependence on human activity, have ministered largely to the indolence and consequent debasement of their possessors, as the histories of many of the most richly favoured countries of the world abundantly testify ; whereas the use of machinery, inasmuch as it is the result of human ingenuity and industry (qualities incompatible with the slothful reposing upon their results), incites to ever-advancing civilisation. In every case in which steam-power has been applied, human labour has been saved in a two-fold, ten-fold, or hundred-fold ratio. We point with intense satisfaction to the completeness with which, under the guidance of one man, it performs what many labouring earnestly at a similar manual operation cannot accomplish ; we smile triumphantly as we compare our own scientific operations with those, primitive and rude, of half-civilised communities, and wonder how the ancient world got on at all without the aid of our new inventions. We complacently compare the Egyptian barge or galley, propelled by scores of rowers and pole-men, with our own river and ocean-going steamers ; or the Hottentot's lumbering waggon, drawn along at the rate of two or three miles an hour by twelve or fourteen pairs of oxen, with the long train of elegant, comfortable carriages rushing along at the rate of forty miles an hour under the superintendence of only three conductors. The labours of the Spanish armourer sink into insignificance when we stand beside the ponderous steam-hammer fashioning coat of mail for a nation's navy. We deplore the loss of time and waste of the labour of the poor Otaheitan or Marquesan clothmaker working at his rough mats, when we see power-looms running off easily and exactly miles of finely finished and comfortable fabrics ; we pity the dusky Hindoo printer who has as much difficulty in executing one spot of his rude pattern as our cylinders overcome in covering fifty yards of calico with an intricate, many-coloured, and beautiful design. But much of this acquisition of power has been used only to increase production. The deck-hand on board the British steam-vessel, the stoker in her hold, work harder far than the boatman on the Nile ; the Kaffir or Hottentot waggon-driver enjoys a life of calm repose compared with the engine-driver or his assistants ; the smith calmly tempering the Toledo blade would look with amazement on the activity and energy of the attendants of the steam-hammer ; the South Sea Islander is used to no such long hours as the women and children of our cotton factories ; and the listless Hindoo would almost as soon be blown from a cannon's mouth at once as spend his life in the active, intelligent operations of machine-printing. It is curious to think that the extensive application of this labour-saving agency has increased the work for human hands to do, not only to the British, its employers, but to an immense portion of the other peoples besides ; the cheap products of steam machinery—the gaudy fabrics, metallic ornaments, cutlery, firearms, &c. (aided by the sturdy canvassing of their vendors, who have advanced from land to land, and penetrated into the most barbarous, running such risks to enlighten the darkened minds of negro, Turcoman, Afghan, Chinaman, and Japanese concerning the merits of our manufactures as missionaries with loftier aim and more valuable merchandise might be proud to emulate), having incited the lazy barbarians to exert themselves in order to procure them. There is no fear of this country settling down into the apathetic indolence of Eastern peoples ; it is the other extreme, in many cases, which we have to fear and avoid.

*To one great end should all conquest over the material world be applied—the freer development of the moral, intellectual, and physical life.* Let this assistance of one of nature's most powerful forces which has been so liberally bestowed, and by furnishing us with which it seems to be one of the most obvious intentions of the Deity to remit a portion of the curse of labour pronounced on Adam's head, and to give to us, the poor overburdened sons of the bleak and barren North, compensation for the want of the rich soil and genial climate of the sunny lands of the Eastern and Western hemispheres, give larger respite from grinding toil. Let this huge material force, so nicely controlled and applied, do away with the long protracted hours of children's labour, and give them time to grow up unharassed, unbent, healthy, and educated. Let it lift up in its hard, iron, adamantine arms from off the delicate, easily crushed body of woman the heavy or prolonged work which enfeebles and distorts her. Let it take from the shoulders of the more stalwart workman a portion of his heavy load of toil, so that what is left may be borne easily and well, and lay up in store for him that which will keep the wolf from his door in the day of sickness which may, and of old age which must, come.

# CHAPTER II.

LEISURE.

(A Lecture delivered on the inauguration of the Renton
Literary Association, 1881.)

IN speaking of the commonwealth which he wished to found
upon Prospero's isle, 'to excel the golden age,' Old Gonzalo
says :—

> No kind of traffic
> Would I admit, no name of magistrate
> Letters should not be known ; riches, poverty,
> And use of service, none ; contract, succession,
> Bourn bound of land, tilth, vineyard, none;
> No use of metal, corn, or wine, or oil ;
> No occupation ; all men idle, all ;
> And women too, but innocent and pure ;
> No sovereignty.
> All things in common nature should produce
> Without sweat or endeavour, treason, felony ;
> Sword, pike, knife, gun, or need of any engine,
> Would I not have ; but nature should bring forth,
> Of its own kind, all foison, all abundance,
> To feed my innocent people.

This poetical description of an entirely labour-free and roving
life, in which—

> They fleet the time carelessly as in the golden world,

after the fashion of the 'banished Duke' and his companions
in the 'Forest of Arden,' is recognised by even the most sanguine Utopians to be impracticable in the present condition of
things, and most undesirable.

Sir Thomas More, in his 'Utopia,' written about 360 years
since, says :—'And if all that languish out their lives in sloth
and idleness (every one of whom consumes as much as any two
of the men that work) were forced to labour, you may easily
imagine that a small proportion of time would serve for doing
all that is either necessary, profitable, or pleasant to mankind,
especially while pleasure is kept within its due bounds.'

Robert Owen, in more modern times, considered that, if
everybody were educated into unselfishness and trained to
work honestly and cheerfully for behoof of everybody else, his

Utopian plan would be accomplished ; and within the last few years Mr. Hoyle, in a book on our 'National Resources and How they are Wasted,' calculates that, if every person did his share, a total of one and a quarter hour's daily labour would suffice to supply us in abundance with all the comforts of life. But in all these calculations there is the fatal ' if.'

In the ideal state of society, now happily the object of much earnest thought and ardent aspiration to men even of strong common sense, in which all the means of life shall be subsidiary to the life itself, labour is to occupy the secondary, well-earned leisure the place of prime importance.

*In speaking of leisure I give to the term its widest scope, in which it embraces all the hours not devoted to the labour pursued to earn a livelihood.*

According to this ideal, leisure, instead merely of a golden hour or two snatched out of the toiling and sleeping twenty-four, should claim them all, with the exception of one or two devoted to labour. Such an amount of leisure (if leisure in their case it can properly be called) is possessed by many barbarous and semi-barbarous tribes. But the prophets of the better order of things predict a very much nobler system of labour, a very much wiser use of leisure than the fitful, hurried snatches of work and long relapses into utter indolence, characteristic of the savage. Combination in labour—recreation in leisure—in both education—these form the key-note of all modern theories. The condition of the civilised working classes of the future, as fondly sketched in them, whilst exempting youth and age from all labour, shall impose upon the adults only a mere modicum of it, and enable them to devote the great portion of their time to ennobling pursuits. And perhaps such a condition will be realised when this eager, toiling, struggling, nineteenth-century British race, which, burrowing, dim-eyed, in the excavations of its mines, has thrown to the surface more mineral than the sun ever before shone upon, which has reared thousands of factories and workshops, and wrought manfully under their murky smoke to supply all the world with tools and clothing, which has covered the land with a network of railways and telegraphs and the sea with steam fleets, shall be succeeded by wiser and less restless generations, reaping the fruits which it has sown, eating the fat of the land which it has reclaimed, riding easily along the smooth ways which it has formed, and likening it to those insects whose lives have been spent in throwing up

C

the gigantic coral reefs which form the basis for the brilliant
superstructure of the vegetable and animal life which crowns
the islands of the Pacific.  But such a condition, if it does
come, must, like everything else that is good and permanent,
be attained by slow but sure progression.

Let us look all round the question, and inquire what should
be the hours of labour and what of leisure under, not ideal,
but actual present circumstances.

To give the most practical idea of the vast labour-saving
powers which have recently been put into our hands, I give
the following quotation from Mr. Hoyle ('Our National Resources, and How they are Wasted,' p. 55) :—' When labour
is rightly applied, and reasonable economy is practised, the
accumulative power of human industry is something marvellous.

' If we take agriculture, in which there has probably been
the least improvement, and where, up to the present time,
machinery has been less applied than in any other department
of labour, one man will cultivate sufficient land to produce
food for the support of at least twenty persons.[1]

' In the manufacture of clothing, owing to the extensive
application of machinery, there is a much greater productive
power.  If we take the production of cotton goods as an example, I find that a cotton mill, containing 800 looms and em-
ploying 667 hands (most of whom are females, and many of
them children from nine to fifteen years of age), will produce
more than 7,000,000 yards of calico per annum.  The average
consumption of calico during the year 1868-9 by the people of
this country was not more than 18 yards per head ; so that,
dividing the quantity produced among the workers, we find
that one person will produce as much cotton cloth as will
supply at least 550 people.  These remarks apply with equal
force to the manufacture of other articles of clothing ; so that,
taking the whole of what man needs in the shape of clothing,
it may be safely asserted that one person will produce as much
as will supply at least 50 people.

' In addition to food and clothing, there only remains to be
provided houses to dwell in and furniture to stock the houses
with.  After carefully investigating this matter, I feel safe in
assuming that to supply these would, at the outside, require no
more labour than is necessary in providing our supply of food;

---

[1] See Note 1 in Appendix to 'Leisure.'

if so, then the total amount of labour needed to provide for our wants will be as follows:—Food, half an hour's labour daily; clothing, fifteen minutes' labour daily; houses, &c., half an hour's labour—that is, assuming every person did his share.'

Within the last fifty years the number of the leisure classes has enormously increased, and it is also calculated that the hours of labour of the working classes have been shortened to the extent of twenty per cent., and the labour-saving appliances have thus been allowed to a large extent to perform their primary and most direct duty. There is no doubt also that wages have increased about 100 per cent., while the purchasing power of money has remained about the same, and they have thus been enabled to improve very much their style of living; and in as far as this has been the case, the great wealth-producing agencies of the century have been allowed to perform their secondary, but no less important, functions. It is very gratifying to be able to note this advancement, and I intend to refer to it more at length in a succeeding chapter on 'Progress'; but, as will be shown in the immediately succeeding article on 'Luxury,' not only the luxury of the rich, but also the luxury of the people, has swallowed up a vast amount of this gain. It will also be shown that this luxury is inherent in the present moral condition of society, and that all effort for the amelioration of the material conditions of the people must begin by elevating the moral tone.

The number of hours of work, which also determine the number of hours of leisure, must be determined only after careful investigation of all existing conditions. There exist, and will do so for a long time, the criminals, the intemperate, the improvident, the foolish, and the reckless. Army, navy, and police must also be maintained, but the better a people becomes there will. be fewer and still fewer of what have been called the non-productive labourers, and more and more scope for leisure to the industrious masses.

At the present time, in the majority of our factories the hours of labour for the adult male population are the same as the law prescribes for women and young persons—viz., fifty-six and a half hours per week. In the great building and engineering trades—that is, amongst masons, bricklayers, carpenters, &c., and all connected with shipbuilding—the hours of labour are only fifty-one hours per week, and many of them are of opinion that they should be still further shortened. The old couplet—

> Seven hours to sleep, to healthful labour seven,
> Ten to the world, and all to heaven,

is even by them seen to be at present impracticable, and the doggrel lines—

> Eight hours' work and eight hours' play,
> Eight hours' sleep and eight shillings a day,

seem to embody the ideas of many British working-men as the practical limit at present to be aimed at. The French workmen are also of this opinion, for at a recent meeting of delegates from forty-eight workmen's societies in Paris, they passed an unanimous resolution to request Government to restrict the hours of labour to eight per day.

In looking at a question of this kind, it is well to look at the hours of actual work of our competitors in the markets of the world. From an interesting paper on the question, ' How can this Country best prepare itself to meet the Increased Competition arising from the spread of Manufacturing Industry in Europe and America ? ' read at the Social Science Congress held in Glasgow, October 1874, by Mr. John Matheson, jun., we learn that the hours of actual work in France, with machinery running, are generally twelve per day ; in Belgium, ten to thirteen per day ; in Prussia, ten to eleven and a half per day ; taking into account a short Saturday where that is given. In Switzerland, although in a few factories the hours do not exceed ten, they vary in general from eleven to thirteen per day, even extending to fourteen in some of the remoter localities. In Russia the working hours are also very long— say, from eleven to thirteen per day, with,.however, a shorter period on Saturdays. In Holland the working hours are as low as ten, and as high as thirteen, most frequently eleven and twelve per day.[1] In the United States the hours of work in mills vary in general from sixty-six to seventy-two per week, being as low as sixty only in a few mills. New York, Maine, and other States run their factories eleven hours a day.

[1] In the succeeding chapter on ' Progress,' it is shown that though the hours of work are so much longer on the Continent, the wages of French working-men are 15 per cent. lower than those of the British ; of German, 24 per cent. ; of Italian, 60 per cent. ; of Spanish, 57 per cent. ; and of Russian, 67 per cent.

The following tabular statement shows (Jeans' 'England's Supremacy,' p. 183) how the hours of labour abroad generally compare with those at home :—

*Hours of Labour in Different Countries.*

| Country | Textile factories Hours per week | Machine factories Hours per week | Percentage of excess over Great Britain | |
|---|---|---|---|---|
| | | | Textile factories | Machine factories |
| Germany . . . . . . . . . | 72 | 60 | 28 | 15 |
| France . . . . . . . . | 72 | 60 | 28 | 15 |
| Austria . . . . . . . . | 66 | 66 | 18 | 27 |
| Russia . . . . . . . . . | 72 to 84 | 72 | 28 to 50 | 38 |
| Switzerland . . . . . . . | 66 | 66 | 18 | 27 |
| Belgium . . . . . . . . | 72 | 62 | 28 | 20 |
| Italy . . . . . . . . . | 69 to 90 | 72 | 23 to 60 | 38 |
| Holland . . . . . . . . | 72 | 64 | 28 | 23 |
| United States . . . . . | 60 | 60 | 8 | 15 |
| United Kingdom . . . . | 56 | 52[1] | ... | ... |

It is necessary to observe, with reference to those figures, that although they are authentic as applied to particular and leading districts, as well as with reference to staple industries, they are not to be taken as applying to all districts and all industries alike.

They will be found, however, to fairly reflect the general condition of the several countries tabulated, with regard to the hours of labour.

And Mr. Mulhall calculates 'that after paying for food, clothing, rent, and taxes, an Englishman has 91 days of the year for leisure or luxuries, an American 75, a Frenchman 69, a German 40, a Russian 14, an Italian 10.'

With the industries of each of these countries we are running a keenly competed race, getting keener and keener each day, by the introduction into them of the best forms of our labour-saving machinery ; and, as a question of mere prudence, it behoves the working classes to consider well whether they are in a position to take it yet still more easily than their competitors. The question of still further reducing the hours of labour is of vital importance, both to them and their employers.

[1] In some machine factories the hours are 54 per week, but in the majority they will be found to average about 52.

As Mr. Dudley Baxter well puts it :—'England's position
is not that of a great landed proprietor, with an assured
revenue, and only subject to occasional loss of crops or hostile
depredations.   It is that of a great merchant, who by immense
skill and capital has gained the front rank and developed an
enormous commerce, but has to support an ever-increasing
host of dependents.   He has to encounter the risks of trade,
and to face jealous rivals, and can only depend on continued
good judgment and fortune and the help of God to maintain
himself and his successors in the foremost place among the
nations of the world.'

As Mr. Jeans sums up on the question, 'the superiority
which has hitherto differentiated English from foreign labour
is every day being diminished.   Such part of our pre-eminence
as has been due to the better command of labour-saving methods
and appliances, to a long course of industrial training, and to
a special knowledge of manufacturing processes, is slowly but
surely being shared by rival nations, and must ultimately be
lost to us.'

The report of the Commission on Depression of Trade, 1886,
states : 'We think also that the increasing severity of the
competition of foreign countries is a matter deserving more
serious attention than it has received at the hands of our
commercial and industrial classes.

'The increasing severity of this competition both in our home
and in neutral markets is especially noticeable in the case of
Germany.   A reference to the reports from abroad will show
that in every quarter of the world the perseverance and enterprise of the Germans are making themselves felt. . In the
actual production of commodities we have now few, if any,
advantages over them ; and in a knowledge of the markets of
the world, a desire to accommodate themselves to local tastes
or idiosyncrasies, a determination to obtain a footing wherever
they can, and a tenacity in maintaining it, they appear to be
gaining ground upon us.' [1]

But, even putting aside this important element of foreign
competition, I have no hesitation in advising working-men,
and particularly trades' unionists, to strive for the three following much more important advantages, before they seek further
to reduce their hours of labour, viz.:—

1st. More leisure for their children—that is, to keep them

[1] See Note 2 in Appendix to ' Leisure.'

longer out of the factory and longer in school—in short, to let them begin life with better health and better education.

2nd. More leisure in the households, by keeping their wives and daughters more from factory work, and letting them attend more to the domestic duties, their natural sphere ; and,

3rd. More leisure for themselves and families in time of sickness and in the decline of life.

With regard to the first two advantages, legislation in this country has effected a wonderful improvement. Women and children in a great many industries are now thoroughly protected from the greed of their employers and the luxurious exactions of their husbands and fathers, as far as the hours of labour are concerned.

The first important Factory Act, regulating the hours of work for women and children, was passed in 1833, and there has been gradual progress in this legislation up to the Factory and Workshops Act of 1878, which has increased the age at which a child is allowed to begin work from eight to ten years, and considers them as children, or half-timers, until they are fourteen years of age, instead of thirteen as before. It has also advanced the age of young persons from sixteen to eighteen years of age, so that every lad is put upon the same footing as a woman until he has attained this age.

Within the last two or three years many articles have been written affirming the decadence of the supremacy of British industry and the gradual submergence of our manufactures by foreign competition, attributed by many economists and employers of labour to the restriction of the hours of labour, enforced by legislation, which, they affirm, besides incurring a smaller output from the workers, also incurs a large diminution of interest on the capital sunk in machinery, which, of course, runs just in proportion to the time of the people employed at it.

Though an employer of labour in which a very large proportion of 'children,' 'young persons,' and ' women ' co-operate, and though, of course, frequently subjected to considerable inconvenience by the operation of the Factory Act referred to, I do not at all concur with those views, but believe that this prosecution of the nation's labour more in accordance with the laws of human physiology will, even from an economic point of view, eventually far more than counterbalance the apparent loss. Factory legislation in this country, championed through the long course of his life by the veteran and highly respected

Earl of Shaftesbury, and others of like noble mind, and resisted
to the very last extremity by many who sought to pose as the
people's benefactors, has conferred great and lasting benefit
upon the British manufacturing population, and, in regulating
production, upon the manufacturers themselves. To those who
can look back upon the time when infants not more than five
or six years of age were carried down to the mills, sleeping in
their fathers' and mothers' arms, and set to begin a long day's
work at six o'clock in the morning, the present, when no child
is allowed to begin work until he is ten years of age, and then
only for five hours per diem, until he is fourteen, seems a time
of wonderful advantage ; and it is questionable if legislation
should meanwhile seek to push further in this direction, except
in extending the scope of the present Act, so as to embrace
many industries which do not come within it, and in which
there is shameful overwork of women and children ; but every
working-man, who can by hook or by crook afford it, should
strive to give his family a better education, and to keep them
longer out of the factory than what is barely prescribed by Act
of Parliament.

The advantages of a good start in life as regards physical
condition tell strongly through all the later years, and a sound
education will not only enable the boys and girls to grow up
into wiser, healthier, and happier men and women,[1] but will
also enable them to work in those enormous and intricate com-
binations of labour, by which the bulk of the industries of the
country is now carried on, with far more advantage to themselves. As individuals, a better education will confer untold
benefit upon them, but as co-operators (to which reference will
be made further on in the chapter on 'The Acquisition of Property by the Working Classes') it is absolutely indispensable
to them.

And whilst thus providing beneficial leisure for his children,
let him not neglect the women of his family. That women
should have the opportunity of earning their own livelihood at
congenial occupations, when dependent upon their own resources or seeking an honest independence apart from married
life, is a great advantage of the present system of things over
the past—an advantage which has been conceded step by step
in many of the manual occupations, where the restriction of
trades' unionism sought to shut them out. In some of the

---

[1] See Note 3 in Appendix to 'Leisure.'

higher callings they have had quite as arduous a battle to fight
to obtain an entrance ; but it is to be hoped that the day is
not far distant when, in all work suited to her, such as the
medical profession (especially as regards the treatment of
women, which is most peculiarly and appropriately within her
sphere) and many of the lighter manual occupations, she will
have a fair field, unhindered by obstacles placed in her way by
a petty self-interest, quite unworthy of the commonest trades
union, not to speak of a learned profession.

But the employment of women in this country has, in many
cases, been carried to great excess, and to the destruction of all
domestic comfort.[1]

'The proportion of adult men now working in English factories is reckoned to be 31 per cent. and of females 51 per cent.
of the entire hands, against 50 per cent. of adult male labour
in France, and 40 per cent. male, with 35 per cent. female, in
Belgium.'[2]

In England, as many as 355,323 out of a total of 586,470,
or 60 per cent. of the whole number engaged in the cotton
industry in 1881, belonged to the female sex.

A very intelligent foreign gentleman, who, as a consul, has
had large experience of the social life of different countries,
our own in particular, stated to me that he considers the
women of the British working classes, owing to their complete
ignorance of the commonest duties of a comfortable household
economy, are more to blame for the wide-spread social degradation than the men.

In Lancashire it is quite common, when a young couple
have been married, for the wife to return to the factory the
next morning to work alongside of her husband, although his
pay is amply sufficient to maintain both ; and this continues
even after they have got children, these unfortunate little
creatures being left to the tender mercies of a general hired
nurse. In our own works we have the wives and daughters
of riveters and others employed in the shipbuilding works of
Dumbarton (restricted by their trades' unions to 51 hours'
labour per week, and earning during this time two to ten
pounds) sent without scruple by their luxurious lords and
masters to do their 56½ hours, the wages which they earn being
often swallowed up along with the larger gains of the men in

---

[1] See Note 4 in Appendix to 'Leisure.'
[2] *Spread of Manufacturing Industry*, by John Matheson, jun.

their weekly debauch, which often curtails their very limited
appointed hours of weekly labour by 18 or 27. It is hardly
necessary to state that in their houses there is not a trace of
domestic comfort. The natural sphere of the married woman
is in her own house, attending to her children and to the
domestic comfort of her husband, and whenever he has the
means to supplement her work in the household by the assistance of a grown-up daughter, let him do so ungrudgingly.
The principal business of life as well as its chief joys are round
the domestic hearth, and money spent in lessening household
drudgery and sweetening and refining home life is the wisest
expenditure that a well-to-do working-man can incur. And I
say to the working-men of Great Britain—to those who do
not work more than fifty-six and a half hours per week—
before they seek further to abridge their own hours of labour,
and seek for what, in many cases, is only time for more luxurious ease and debauchery, let them devote themselves to the
manlier, nobler, more chivalric task of better educating their
children, and enfranchising their wives and daughters with that
leisure which would tend so much to the comfort, refinement,
and happiness of their homes ; and though, for nothing else,
they should not seek to lessen by one iota their present moderate hours of labour.

But, in addition to the better education of their children
and improvement of the domestic arrangements of their wives
and daughters, there is a third and very important object
which they should strive to attain before speaking of lessening
their work, and that is more leisure for themselves and their
wives in times of sickness and in the decline of life. Everyone who is familiar with the working classes must know the
fearful privations to which many families are exposed by the
even temporary sickness of the bread-winner. Living, as the
saying goes, from hand to mouth, with no thought save to
provide for the necessities of the hour, an unexpected prostration of a few months by sickness has reduced many a family
to the direst destitution, involved such a sacrifice of clothing
and furniture, and hung round their necks such a load of debt
as to cripple them for life. There is no sadder sight than that
of an aged couple, who have done good service to the community in their day and generation, but who have lived as if the
strength and skill of youth and middle age should never depart,
reduced to a state of abject dependence upon grudging relatives,

or forced to take shelter in that most unwelcome of asylums —the poor's house.

Working-men should not attempt to ignore the fact that they are subject to a certain percentage of sickness, increasing steadily as they grow older, and that their capacity for remunerative employment generally terminates long before death.

The annual average days of sickness per inhabitant in this country between the ages of 21 and 30 is 5·5 ; between 31 and 40, 7·1 ; between 41 and 50, 10·8 ; and between 51 and 60, 20·2.

In the United Kingdom, excluding children, there are 372 millions of days of sickness, involving a loss of labour equal to 36½ million pounds sterling, being an average loss of 21s. per head.[1]

Now I wish to impress upon you most emphatically that leisure in times of sickness—that is, the leisure unharassed by the petty cares of providing for the morrow, and the sweet leisure of a happy convalescence, also that beautiful leisure of old age in which the aged husband can totter out and in at his own sweet will, to fulfil the easy tasks which are his of choice, or sit by the fireside with his partner for life just as they wish—can rest only upon the possession of property.

In the chapter on 'The Acquisition of Property by the Working Classes,' which is to follow, which shows to them that property means independence, I recommend at length the acquisition, first of all, of the proprietorship of their own houses, and, in the second place, of an interest in the distributive co-operative societies which are now so common throughout the country, as being generally the best investment for their money.

But along with this, and sometimes where the circumstances are peculiar, in place of this the workmen should provide against the day of bad health and old age by contributing regularly to one of the many workmen's friendly societies which, fortunately, have been so much on the increase of late, by depositing in the savings' bank, or in the regular payments necessary to secure life annuities, either from the Post Office or one of those admirable insurance companies which lay themselves out for this business.

Appended is a note of the Post Office system of life

---

[1] Mulhall's *Dictionary of Statistics.*

annuities, which appears in a small pamphlet by the Right Hon. Henry Fawcett, M.P., Her Majesty's Postmaster-General, who takes such an intelligent interest in all economical questions.

## How Annuities can be Bought.

*Life Annuities.*—At all the post offices where lives can be insured annuities can also be bought in any of the following ways, provided that the person for whom the annuity is bought is not less than 10 years of age.

1. *Immediate Life Annuities.*—By the payment of a lump sum an annuity not exceeding 50*l.* can be secured for life. Thus, a man who is between 30 and 31 years of age may secure an annuity of 10*l.* (equal to about 3*s.* 10*d.* a week) by the payment of a lump sum of 185*l.* 1*s.* 8*d.*, and if he is 50, by the payment of 136*l.* 9*s.* 2*d.*

As it is found that a woman's expectation of life is better than a man's, a woman between 30 and 31 purchasing an annuity of 10*l.* would have to pay 198*l.* 17*s.* 6*d.*, and at the age of 50, 156*l.* 7*s.* 6*d.*

2. *Deferred Life Annuities.*—By the payment of a lump sum an annuity to commence at a particular age may be purchased. Thus, a man between 30 and 31 may purchase an annuity of 10*l.*, to commence when he reaches the age of 60, by the payment of a lump sum of 24*l.* 3*s.* 4*d.*, or by an annual payment till he reaches the age of 60 of 1*l.* 8*s.* 4*d.* A woman between 30 and 31 can purchase an annuity of 10*l.* to commence when she reaches the age of 60, by the payment of a lump sum of 32*l.* 8*s.* 4*d.*, or by the annual payment till she reaches the age of 60 of 1*l.* 17*s.* 6*d.*

If persons who wish to purchase annuities to commence on their reaching the age of 60 prefer to do so by monthly payments instead of by annual payments, they can. A man between 30 and 31 can, by the payment of 8*s.* a month until he is 60, secure an allowance of 2*l.* 7*s.* 3*d.* a month when he reaches that age ; and a woman between 30 and 31 can, by the payment of 8*s.* a month until she is 60, secure an allowance of 1*l.* 16*s.* 7*d.* a month when she reaches that age.

3. *Deferred Life Annuities.—Money Returnable.*—If a person is willing to pay a larger sum down, or to make larger annual payments, the money which is so spent in the purchase of an annuity to commence at 60 will be returned if the person dies before 60, or is unable or unwilling to continue the annual

payments until he is 60. Thus, a man between 30 and 31 may buy an annuity of 10*l.* of this kind, to commence when he is 60, by the payment of a lump sum of 40*l.* 9*s.* 2*d.*, or by an annual payment until he is 60 of 2*l.* 0*s.* 10*d.* ; and a woman between 30 and 31 may purchase an annuity of 10*l.*, to commence when she is 60, by a payment down of 47*l.* 0*s.* 10*d.*, or by an annual payment until she is 60 of 2*l.* 7*s.* 6*d.*

To show the advantages of this kind of annuity, the case may be taken of a man between 30 and 31 commencing to purchase a deferred annuity of 10*l.* of this kind by annual payments of 2*l.* 0*s.* 10*d.* : if he died when he was between 50 and 51, or if from any other cause he ceased to make the payments, he or his family would receive back all the money he had paid in the annual premiums during the previous 20 years, viz., 40*l.* 16*s.* 8*d.*

If persons wish to buy annuities of the kind just described by monthly payments they can do so. Thus, a man between 30 and 31 can, by the payment of 8*s.* a month until he is 60, secure an allowance of 1*l.* 14*s.* 2*d.* per month on reaching that age ; and a woman between 30 and 31 can, by the payment of 8*s.* a month till she is 60, secure an allowance of 1*l.* 9*s.* 4*d.* a month on reaching that age.

A small fee is chargeable on annuities in order to meet the working expenses.

Persons who wish to find out on what terms they can insure their lives, or buy any of the annuities described above, can, on applying at a post office, obtain tables which will give them full information.

The Post Office Guide, which can be purchased for a small sum at any post office, also gives much detailed information on the subjects treated of in the foregoing pages, as well as on all other branches of Post Office business.

The Prudential Assurance Company, which has an enormous industrial branch, guarantees an annuity of 12*l.* on attaining the age of 60, and a sum of 12*l.* to be paid at death, either before or after the annuity has commenced, for a payment of 9*d.* per week in the case of males, and 10*d.* in the case of females, beginning at 20 years of age, the annuity to be paid in instalments of 1*l.* on the first day of each calendar month. And I am glad to say that this form of insurance is increasing at a very rapid rate amongst our working classes.[1]

---

[1] See Note 5 in Appendix to 'Leisure.'

To see the honest workman carefully tended and liberally nourished during his time of sickness, and to see him sitting peacefully and cheerfully under the shade of his own vine and fig tree when time has weakened the muscles of his brawny arm, though not destroyed his capacity for serene enjoyment of life, is a consummation devoutly to be wished for, and is within the grasp of a vast number by their simply abstaining from unnecessary luxuries. This will be taken up more at length in the chapter on 'Luxury,' and I will now content myself by stating that I have known a great many intemperate workmen exposed to destitution in sickness and old age, but very few amongst the temperate.

The Venerable Archdeacon Farrar goes the length of 'considering that there is hardly a pauper in England who has not wasted on intoxicants enough to have secured him long ago a freehold house and a good annuity.' But we must always bear in mind that, amid the exigencies of trade and in the sore battle of life, many good and temperate workmen go to the wall through no faults of their own, and for their sakes alone our charitable organisations are well worthy of support.[1] The opinion of the Venerable Archdeacon, however, holds good regarding the majority of those requiring eleemosynary aid. As directly, but more inevitably, than our criminal population by the judge's sentence, are multitudes of our working classes condemned to (what is virtually) imprisonment and hard labour for life by the inexorable consequences of their own luxurious appetites.

The other day I had an appeal for assistance from the wife of an aged tradesman in destitute circumstances, who admitted that during the vigour of his manhood he was in the habit of regularly saving a pound per month for six months, when he had a severe debauch, in which the whole of the savings were dissipated, and then he returned to his work just to repeat the same course. The twelve pounds per annum thus luxuriously wasted, if it had been invested prudently, as has been shown, would have provided for them both comfortably during any sickness, and furnished them with a snug annuity which would have raised them beyond the reach of want. Even in the case of moderate drinkers, it is well worth their while to

---

[1] 'There be just men, unto whom it happeneth according to the work of the wicked; again, there be wicked men, to whom it happeneth according to the work of the righteous.'—Eccles. viii. 14.

curtail in this respect, for the sake of future ease and competency.

Many workmen are under the impression that their hours of labour may be indefinitely abridged and their pay remain the same, but, *cæteris paribus*, less work means less production and less pay. I have pointed out three good and noble objects, any one of which should be preferred by the adult workman before a further reduction of his hours of labour. I refer, of course, to those who are not working more than fifty-six and a half hours per week. The time, I trust, will come when, having secured a liberal education for his children, a happy domestic life for his wife and daughters, a solid platform of property on which he himself can repose in sickness and old age, he will be able to advance boldly and manfully to claim a still further measure of well-earned leisure, a larger share of the fruits of industry by a better adjustment of his economic relationship ; but, in the meantime, let him work patiently for those things which should be to him of primary importance.

With fifty-six and a half hours of work per week, and leaving out of view the inestimable boon of the Sabbath, that day of purest, noblest, happiest leisure, and which, when rightly used, confers such priceless moral and physical benefits, and supposing that you require three hours for meals and eight hours for sleep per diem (some may require more and some less, but the unwisest of all economies is to abridge the natural hours of sleep), you have twenty-one hours of solid leisure per week with about a fortnight's holiday per annum added.

The natural and most profitable recreation for the manual labourer is in the exercise of his intellectual along with the resting of his physical faculties, and a portion of your leisure can be spent in no better way than that which you are proposing for yourselves in the cultivation and expansion of your intellectual being. If you, as a literary association, can so permeate the mass of the inhabitants of this village, as to induce them to apply a portion of their leisure to the study of intellectual and moral subjects, each of you inducing some less enthusiastic companion to swell your ranks, and so increase the scope of this society's influence that the bulk of the young men of Renton should be included in it, what a transformation should we not behold in its every aspect ! Instead of the brawling, drunken revelry so often witnessed in our streets, we should have a sober, respectable, and intelligent community of young men growing up amongst us, into whose hands the guidance of all the affairs belonging to the place must naturally fall, and who, along with the improvement of themselves, would most assuredly effect the improvement of all their surroundings ; and I trust that this district, which is intimately associated with some of the best names in English literature—as witness Smollett, the poet, novelist, and historian, and Thomas Campbell, the poet—will yet send forth from the ranks of this very literary society of working-men some who will emulate their famous predecessors in those literary accomplishments which have so much distinguished it. From the ranks of the working classes have come some of the foremost men in manufacture, commerce, art, and literature. There is no reason why some of you also should not come to the front.

But if your intellectual exercise does not confer upon you distinction, it will at least give you (what is better) an intelligent and pleasant interest in and sympathy with the thoughts of the leading minds of your country, and a clearer insight into those things which more nearly concern yourselves. The study of ‘social science,’ of those branches of it which concern the advancement of the industrial classes into a superior economic relationship, should form part of the study of all working-men’s literary associations.

A portion of this twenty-one hours of leisure, belonging to the young women, could be spent in no better way than in securing a higher knowledge of the domestic arts, such as needlework, cookery, &c., which are so essential to the comfort of a home, but which in the works there is no opportunity of acquiring.

The education of our young women in practical domestic economy is of the very first importance, not only for themselves, but for the physical comfort and moral tone of the whole community.

And now a word or two regarding the leisure classes. All *absolute leisure—that is, leisure enjoyed without the necessity for any work to gain a livelihood*—is based on the possession of property (and increased leisure for the working classes must be based upon this too), and one of the consequences of the enormous increase of property, resulting from the introduction of steam machinery, has been the steady increase of those whose lives are entirely spent in leisure. In 1800 there were in Britain 36,000 families of gentry with income of 28,000,000*l* sterling; in 1883, 222,000 families with income of 333,000,000*l*., but there are a great many more, probably 100,000 to 200,000 families, not included in this class, who do not require to work for their subsistence.

In the following chapter on ' Luxury ' I will endeavour to show how that, in proportion as the working classes acquire a larger share of property by higher intelligence and morality, labour and leisure will also be much more evenly distributed ; the numbers of those enabled to lead the lives of luxurious sinecures through the present concentration of wealth being, perhaps, though not necessarily, curtailed ; but certainly the leisure of the industrious classes, in childhood, in sickness, and in old age, augmented.

The advantages of the position held by some 300,000 or 400,000 families in Great Britain, in which a livelihood has not to be earned, but in which the whole life is that of leisure, for giving command over all accomplishments and refinements are undoubted ; but the leisure classes are now being more and more impressed with the idea that property has its duties as well as its rights and advantages. Their first duty (after those which they owe to themselves) is to strive as much as lies in their power to ameliorate the condition of the toiling millions whose industry enables their capital to fructify. Thousands of them, happily, from the highest peers in the realm downwards, are devoting a great part of their leisure to this noble purpose, and let us hope that their number will go on constantly increasing.

The manual labouring class I have advised to seek for recreation in their leisure hours in intellectual exercise. The leisure class would find in the acquisition and practice of many of the handicrafts recreation, instruction, and improvement, of which at present they have no idea. In no other way would they so well know the value of labour, the sweets of leisure, the cost of production and the modes of just expenditure. In no other way would they find so much improvement for their bodies and rest for their minds. And this is equally applicable to the ladies amongst them. Jean Ingelow, in a letter to Lucy Stone, says ' that she takes a keen interest in one problem which women have to work out, viz., how domestic work is to be combined with high culture. So long as household work is thought degrading—and nowhere is this

D

so much so as in America—there never can be anything like universal education ; there must always be some who work all their lives because others will not work at all.   It is one of the great things that you Americans, I believe, are raised up for, to teach the world how this is to be done ; but the teachers can never be those who are poor—they must be those who are not obliged to work at all.   How to make clear starching and ironing graceful and pretty occupations—and such they were thought by our great-great-grandmothers— how to keep and to assist even in a kitchen without the least sense of being lowered or the slightest personal deterioration, might surely be managed if women gave their mind to it.'

The Germans, like the ancient Hebrews, have a very strong opinion as to the advantages of acquiring a trade, so much so that all their princes have to be apprenticed to some trade or other.   Writing a good many years ago, the Berlin corre· spondent of the 'Times' says :—'Speaking of royal usages in this country, I must not leave unmentioned that Prince Henry, the second son of the Princess Royal, has been apprenticed to a bookbinder.   According to immemorial practice, all the youthful scions of this dynasty have to learn a handicraft as part of their education.   It is supposed, and I believe justly, that the mechanical skill acquired in these pursuits is a valuable means of fostering thrifty habits and accurate observation. His reigning Majesty, if I am not mistaken, is by trade a glazier ; his son and heir, I believe, a carpenter.'

In the material world there has been left, as it were, a certain amount of resistance beautifully proportioned to the human faculties, and in the overcoming of which these faculties attain their highest improvement.   The conquering of this resistance with your own hands gives firmness and skill to your muscles, insight and justness of perception to your mind, calmness and steadiness of purpose to your soul.   'Muscular Christianity,' so much valued in the present day, is to be acquired of a higher type from the prosecution of some active handicraft, implying steady, resolute, and intelligent conquest over the material world, than from many of the showy gymnastic exercises recommended for its attainment.   And this we know, that the loftiest thought and purest morality to which the world has ever listened proceeded from the lips of One, whose sublime yet practical sagacity and deep insight into the nature of man and his surroundings, we cannot doubt, grew with the knowledge and practice of His trade as a carpenter, and whose will acquired the calm strength necessary for the most heroic and unshrinking self-sacrifice as His physical frame became firmed and knit by manly toil.

---

# CHAPTER III.

## LUXURY.

THE following chapter on 'Luxury' appeared in 'Fraser's Magazine' for October 1872, under Froude's editorship, and attracted a considerable amount of attention at the time. Mr. E. D. Girdlestone made an epitome of it, and published it as one of his famous Weston-super-Mare penny tracts. It was otherwise also frequently referred to.

For the most of the statistics upon which it was based, I was indebted (in addition to 'Government Returns ') to the admirable statements of Mr. Dudley Baxter, Professor Leone Levi, and Mr. Wm. Hoyle, regarding 'National Income and Taxation,' 'The Wages and Earnings of the Working Classes,' and 'Our National Resources, and How they are Wasted.'

In this edition I have brought the statistics as nearly as possible up to date, and for these statistics I have been indebted to the new edition of Professor Leone Levi's ' Wages and Earnings of the Working Classes,' to Mr. Mulhall's 'Dictionary of Statistics' and ' History of Prices,' to the ' Essays in Finance ' (2nd series), by Mr. Giffen, President of the Statistical Society, and to Mr. William Hoyle's ' Our National Drink Bill for 1884.'

With this exception the chapter appears very nearly as at first published.

About the time that this chapter was first written the luxuriousness of the Country, both as regards wealthy luxuries and popular luxuries, seems to have attained its culminating-point in many directions, and there has been very great improvement since then, the principal items of which are noted and commented upon in the immediately following chapter on ' Progress.'

For those who wish to make the comparison, the statistics of the luxury of 1870 are given in the Appendix[1] as they originally appeared in the article.

The term 'Luxury ' has hitherto been used by political economists in a vague and indefinite sense. This is, as far as I know, the first attempt to place it on a scientific basis, and to define it with exactness, and is submitted as an original contribution to the science of Political Economy. It is one of the most important

[1] See Note 1 in Appendix to ' Luxury.'

subjects coming within the scope of this science, and a due consideration of it would, I believe, help very much to elucidate many of those perplexing social problems which are at present attracting universal attention.

This treatise, instead of indiscriminately stigmatising all luxuries, seeks to point out the great and important ends which many of them have subserved (and are subserving) in elevating the general standard of living, but at the same time also the evils resulting from vicious luxuriousness.

SOME things, such as alcohol and menial service, from their very nature, must always remain luxuries ; others, such as air, water, and food, are no less absolutely necessaries ; but, with the exception of *positive luxuries* and the prime necessaries, luxury and necessary are terms entirely relative to the degree of civilisation, properly so-called. Hunger and thirst, and the other natural physical wants, sharply denote to us the *prime necessaries*. In savage life they also define as luxuries the few things in use beyond their simple boundaries. Civilisation complicates the subject. Every advance in the arts of life adds to the list of luxuries. It also subtracts from it by transforming some of them into what Dr. Chalmers styles ' *second necessaries*,' of which books are the supreme type.

But while the scope of these terms is thus dependent upon the degree of knowledge attained of the arts of life, and industry in applying them—in a word, upon *production*—it is even more so upon the degree of morality which controls and directs the labour, and regulates the *distribution* of the products ; for a nation of a so-called very inferior civilisation, but with a superior morality to guide its ruder work into proper channels, and wisely to distribute its smaller means, may have a higher standard of living—the mass of its populace enjoy to a far greater extent the real necessaries and comforts of life—than another of a much further ' advanced ' (?) but more vicious civilisation.

I define as luxuries EVERYTHING IN USE BEYOND THE PRESENT PROPER SCOPE OF WORKMEN'S AVERAGE INCOME. Professor Leone Levi ('Wages and Earnings of the Working Classes,' pp. 2 and 3) estimates the number of the manual-labour class in these islands at 26,000,000 with an annual income of 521,000,000*l.*,[1] giving a proportional income of about

---

[1] Mulhall's estimate of the income of the working classes is 447,000,000*l.* ; Levi's 521,000,000*l.*, leaving a difference of 74,000,000*l.* ; but Mulhall only gives 4,629,000 families as belonging to the working

20*l*. per head, or 93*l*. per family.[1] We have here the statistics for easily and correctly drawing the line between the necessary and the luxury of our present political economy, which treats of things as they are. Everything, with the exception of positive luxuries, included in the style of living which about 36*s*. per week, judiciously expended, would enable a family of from four to five persons to maintain, is a necessary ; everything beyond that a luxury.

In China, Hindostan, and other Eastern countries, there has been, for centuries, a fixed line of demarcation between luxury and necessary—a stereotyped economical condition. It has been entirely different with the progressive European civilisation of the last few centuries, and especially of the present ; and the modern science of political economy demonstrates the important place held by luxuries amongst the civilising agencies. It shows that the desire to possess them has been, and is, one of the most powerful incentives to industry and invention, and that, but for their prior introduction as luxuries by the rich, many of our most valuable necessaries would never have had existence. The rich sought to have well-lighted houses, and the use of glass is now universal ; wealth must ride in carriages, and macadamised highways now stretch into every corner of the land. A vast number of the familiar conveniences of modern times have had a similar origin, but the results of the invention of the art of printing furnish the finest example in all history. Before it, a book was a life-work, and lay, a guarded treasure, in royal or monastic library, one of the costliest luxuries. The growing taste of the rich of the Middle Ages for this most laudable form of luxury induced the invention, and so encouraged its working and improvement that literature is now universal, and books are in all homes. To the general diffusion of many similar things which are now luxuries (that is, to the making of them necessaries) social science looks forward as one of the great means of refining and civilising the masses. These favourable opinions on the subject, however, are of very recent origin ; for, unfortunately, *Luxuriousness*—the excessive use of luxuries by the rich, and an exactly corresponding want of

classes, whilst Levi's calculation is 5,600,000. Mr. Giffen estimates the income at 550,000,000*l*., and Mr. Jeans at 535,000,000*l*., but as Professor Leone Levi has gone into the matter most minutely, I accept his figure for my calculations.

[1] See Note 2 in Appendix to ' Luxury.'

necessaries by the poor—has been the most general and conspicuous form in which they have figured in the ancient civilisations—a chief cause of their decline and extinction.

' The luxury of the rich, or their more refined mode of living, was regarded by the ancient moralists as an evil of the first magnitude,'[1] and the sacred writers are scathing in their denunciations of it. The instinctive popular feeling of all ages, attaching to luxuries the twofold stigma of being wrung from the oppression of the poor, and enervating and debasing the rich, finds noble expression also in the words of the great poet of the English Commonwealth :—

> If every just man, that now pines with want,
> Had but a moderate and beseeming share
> Of that which lewdly-pamper'd luxury
> Now heaps upon some few with vast excess,
> Nature's full blessings would be well dispensed
> In unsuperfluous, even proportion,
> And she no whit encumber'd with her store.[2]

The national bard of Scotland, in ' The Cotter's Saturday Night,' one of his noblest poems, apostrophising his native country, says :—

> O Scotia, my dear, my native soil,
> For whom my warmest wish to Heaven is sent,
> Long may thy hardy sons of rustic toil
> Be blest with health, and peace, and sweet content !
> And, oh ! may Heaven their simple lives prevent
> From luxury's contagion, weak and vile !
> Then, howe'er crown and coronets be rent,
> A virtuous populace may rise the while,
> And stand, a wall of fire, around their much-loved isle.

That the earth shall yield increase to the labour of the tiller, not only sufficient to support himself, but many others also, and set them free to engage in other occupations, is one of the many beneficent adaptations of the physical world to human capacities—the solid material foundation of art, science, and civilisation itself. By uniting and directing its labour to take advantage of this arrangement, has every civilised nation emerged from barbarism ; and in exact accordance with the extent and power of its morality has been the character of the structure which it has reared. Civilisation and luxuriousness rest upon this same basis. In every civilisation the peasant and craftsman have advanced in the comforts and refinements

---

[1] Smith's *Wealth of Nations.*　　　　[2] Milton's *Comus.*

of life but little beyond the condition of their savage ancestry, who wrought every man to supply his own wants only ; while the powerful few have, by the very moral constitution of the society in which they existed, appropriated to their own luxuriousness the surplus labour and value gained by union, which should have gone to the civilising of the whole mass. There has never yet been seen an entirely civilised people. The Egyptian, the Greek, the Roman civilisations, so called— even the Hebrew, superior to them all, and at one part of its career approaching in some respects nearer to perfection than any since produced—were all founded upon the enforced slavery of a portion of their peoples ; while modern civilisations rest upon the self-imposed helotry of their industrial populations.

Luxuriousness is the first evidence, and one of the chief causes, of a people's degeneracy. From the nature of civilisation it has always been its peculiar bane. Its results have been conspicuous in the great events of the world's history—in the enervation and overthrow of once warlike races, in the complete extinction of mighty nations. Civilisation advanced among many ancient peoples, if not as rapidly as of late, at least with swift and steady pace ; but its wealth, instead of equably diffusing itself, and thereby invigorating every member of the body-politic, rushed in swollen, unhealthy tide to the head, thence to pour back (in payment for luxuries) an impure and vitiating stream, until, like a bloated, epicurean apoplectique, the diseased organisation of itself collapsed suddenly and irrecoverably, or shrivelled up at the mere touch of a hardy, barbarous race, which, sweeping away, along with the corruption, all the improvements of centuries—the art and science which it was too ignorant to appreciate—settled down upon the rich domains of its beaten foes—whose ancestors in the same savage condition, and mayhap in like manner expelling others, had there in remote ages pitched their tents—to run in all probability a race the same, and with a goal not different.

We profess a religion teaching a loftier morality-than that of ancient nationalities, and which should most assuredly lead to higher social and economical results ; and if Christianity is to be aught else than a name, it has yet to grapple with and overthrow that which has hitherto formed, and still forms, the chief bane and weakness of all progress in wealth.

It may be laid down as an axiom of political economy that

*luxuriousness is exactly proportionate to inequality in the pos-session of property;* in the first place because the vicious luxury of the masses is a great cause of the undue concentra-tion of wealth, and in the second because this wealth has power to direct labour into any channel which it may see fit ; and as long as men in such a society have the power they direct it to the production of luxuries ; for, in addition to the craving of effeminate natures for luxuries for their own sake, ambition in those of higher type ruthlessly demands them for the sake of social distinction ; and there is practically no limit to the number whom only one man would employ entirely for his own personal gratification. The most complete inequality in the possession of property is to be found in the institution of slavery, and wherever slavery has existed has been found incorporated with it the grossest and most corrupt luxurious-ness.

Centralisation has been one of the distinguishing features of the nineteenth century. Its material progress has, of ne-cessity, aided and palpably demonstrates this. Countless lines traverse the circumambient air for union of thought ; the solid surface of the earth is girded with converging iron, along which sweep myriads of men and untold wealth to the great city centres ; and, underneath the trodden surface, system inter-lacing system distributes to all homes from common reservoirs. Individual isolated action is impossible.

'The population of the country is, in round numbers, 36,000,000, and of these less than 3,000,000 persons are de-voted to producing the food of the United Kingdom—a dis-proportion unparalleled in the present state of Europe, or in the past history of the world. From 1811 to 1841 the popula-tion increased by 7,000,000, and at the same time agriculturists decreased by 300,000. Coming down to a later period, from 1851 to 1861 the population still increased, though not to any large extent, and the agricultural population diminished by 400,000, and all that tide of life flowed from the agricultural districts into the manufacturing towns.' ('In 1851 the rural population comprised 49 per cent. of the population ; in 1881, 40·4 per cent. In 1851 those engaged in agricultural occupa-tions amounted to 21·8 per cent. of the workers of the United Kingdom ; in 1871, 14·6 per cent., and in 1881 only about 11½ per cent., whilst the average for Europe is 55 per cent.'— Mulhall's ' Dictionary of Statistics.')

But concentration of property has resulted to a far greater

extent than that of population, the most startling proof of which is to be found in the statistics of the possession of the land.

'The new Domesday Book showed that the 33,000,000 acres forming the area of England and Wales were held by 972,836 persons. But of the total area, 5,386,913 acres, or more than 16 per cent., was held by 293 proprietors, while only 4,297,754 acres, or 13 per cent., was held by owners who had under 100 acres each. Again, of the 972,836 owners of land in England and Wales, there are no less than 703,289 who own less than one acre each, their total holding being only 151,148 acres, or an average of one-fifth of an acre per head, while a single duke owns 30,000 acres more than the whole of these 703,289 persons.'—Jeans' 'England's Supremacy,' pp. 55-56.

Mulhall's 'Dictionary of Statistics' (1884) gives the number of landed proprietors with holdings above five acres in the United Kingdom as 180,000, being one-half per cent. of the population, whilst France has 9 per cent., and the average of Europe is 8 per cent.

A similar inequality of distribution is the rule with all other property. The total real and personal property of the United Kingdom is estimated by Mr. Mulhall in his 'Dictionary of Statistics' at 8,720,000,000*l.*, of which the working classes own the paltry estimated sum of 430,000,000*l.*,[1] only a twentieth part of the whole, which gives about 16*l.* 10*s.* per head, or 75*l.* per family, while the upper classes own property to the value of 8,290,000,000*l.*, being upwards of 830*l.* per head, or about 3,750*l.* per family—that is, averaging their whole property as belonging to 10,000,000 ; but at least four-fifths of this entire property belongs, as will subsequently be shown, to some 750,000 persons, who, with their families, number less than 3½ millions, and constitute the real upper classes, whose average property is about 2,000*l.* per head, or 8,800*l.* per family. The separation between labour and capital is thus seen to be very marked. With the fervid, disciplined industry, so powerfully and skilfully supplemented by machinery, which this concentrated wealth has at command, the result is such a gigantic system of luxury as has never before existed in the world's history. The extent of this luxury I propose to measure by the statistics which we have at command regarding the incomes of the various classes of society.

---

[1] See *Acquisition of Property by the Working Classes*, p. 87.

The following is an estimate of the income of the entire
population of the United Kingdom for the year ending
March 31, 1884 :—

| | £ |
|---|---|
| Schedule A. | |
| In respect of lands, tenements, &c. . . . | 175,555,583 |
| Schedule B. | |
| In respect of the occupation of lands[1] (nett amount) . . . . . . | 33,460,049 |
| Schedule C. | |
| In respect of annuities, dividends, &c. . | 40,580,571 |
| Schedule D. | |
| In respect of professions, trades, employments, railways, mines, ironworks, &c. . | 252,022,971 |
| Schedule E. | |
| In respect of public offices . . . | 29,510,323 |
| | 531,129,500 |
| Unreturned profits under Schedule D. . | 70,000,000 |
| The 120l. a year excused to incomes between 150l. and 400l. . . . . | 40,000,000 |
| Incomes not charged to Income Tax . | 180,000,000 |
| Total Income of upper classes [2] . . | 821,000,000 |
| Income of the manual-labour classes, estimated by Mr. Levi . . . . | 521,000,000 |
| Total National Income . . . . | 1,342,000,000 |

The number of the middle and higher classes is estimated
at 10,000,000. Deduct the amount which, at the politico-
economical standard already fixed, these 10,000,000 have to
expend for necessaries, viz., 200,000,000l., and the balance of
*six hundred and twenty million pounds sterling represents the
gross expenditure for the luxuries of wealth.*

But the result is far more astounding when it can be shown
that of these 620,000,000l., 550,000,000l. are expended for the
entire and special luxury of about 750,000 families, or less
than 3½ millions of the population. From careful investigation
of recent Government returns and other sources of information,
I calculate the gross number of persons with incomes of upwards of 200l. a year to be not more than 700,000, and their
aggregate income 620,000,000l., of which about 200,000,000l.
is appropriated by about 12,000 persons, about 160,000,000l.
by 88,000 persons, and about 260,000,000l. by 600,000 persons.
But in order that there may not be the least appearance of

[1] Deductions under Schedule B. 32,054,131l.
[2] See Note 3 in Appendix to 'Luxury.'

overstatement in what is to follow, let us say that this income
of 620,000,000*l.* is drawn by 50,000 persons more, viz.,
750,000. This gives an average of about 185*l.* per head, or
830*l.* per family, while the remainder of those who belong to
the so-called upper and middle classes—over 6,500,000, with
an income of about 200,000,000*l.*—possess an average of living
very little higher than the manual-labour class, while thousands of them, including a large staff of clerks, shopmen,
&c., are expected to keep up appearances which render their
lot one of far greater hardship than that of the artisan.

The amount which this 6½ millions of the population consume in the luxuries of wealth is about 70,000,000*l.*, giving
them 11*l.* per head, or 50*l.* per family, of a living above the
line of necessaries.

They form a numerous and most important section of our
splendid social gradation, coming in immediately above the
manual-labour class.

These 70,000,000*l.* fall as distinctly within the scope of
the politico-economical definition of the luxuries of wealth, as
those of the classes above them, but as they constitute only
about one-ninth part of the total luxuries of wealth, and are
distributed over such a large area, I do not intend to again
refer to them in detail, but will confine my remarks to the
550,000,000*l.* expended for luxuries by the classes above them.

To supply with necessaries this 750,000, who, with their families, number less than 3½ millions of the population, and constitute the real upper classes, would require about 70,000,000*l.*,
thus leaving their total expenditure for luxuries 550,000,000*l.*

Before giving an estimate of the principal elements which
go to make up this grand total of 550,000,000*l.*, I premise
that, in the consideration of this subject, though the industrial
population, at first sight, would seem naturally to divide into
these two great classes—those who produce necessaries and
those who produce luxuries—yet it is much easier to classify
the products than the producers, and, judging by the standard
already fixed, to say of certain things that they are necessaries
and of others that they are luxuries, than to say of the majority of workers that they belong to either class ; for the same
workshop often turns out together luxury and necessary, and
the same means of distribution often serves for both. The
same agricultural labourer often tills the ground to produce
the prime necessary of food and the dangerous luxury of
alcohol. A mason building an artisan's cottage is certainly

engaged in producing an important necessary, but the same man, doing his small share towards the erection of the millionaire's palatial edifice, is aiding to construct one of the costliest luxuries. The stately ship contains the gorgeous saloon and the miserable forecastle, and no mere human calculation can rank exactly into their respective classes the thousands who labour in our shipbuilding yards, or man the vessels which are launched from them. It may, however, be safely affirmed that, at least, *the half of the whole labour of the United Kingdom is for the production of the luxuries of wealth.*

We arrive at this conclusion from the following calculations :—

Of the 175,000,000*l.* in Schedule A about 60,000,000*l.*, in round numbers, is for the rent of land. Assuming that the land is used for the benefit of the different classes of society in proportion to their incomes, 28,000,000*l.* will represent the value of that portion used for the upper classes. Deduct from this what has to be set down to them as necessary (less than an eleventh of the whole)—say 5,000,000*l.*—and the value of that portion of it devoted to purposes of wealthy luxury cannot amount to less than 23,000,000*l.* Treating the 33,000,000*l.* in Schedule B, 'in respect of the occupation of lands,' in the same manner, we must add 12,000,000*l.* to this amount, making a total of 35,000,000*l.*

The most notorious feature in this luxurious application and occupation of the land is the large extent of it entirely devoted to the chase. It is calculated that at least a seventh part of the reclaimable land of Great Britain remains in a state of nature, chiefly that it may serve as the occasional playground of its few owners. A tenth part of Scotland, equal to about 1,380,000 acres,[1] is appropriated to deer forest alone. Much of this land was at one time arable, and has been, in quite recent times, depopulated in a manner not much less arbitrary than that by which William the Conqueror, who, the old Saxon Chronicle tells us, 'loved the high deer as if he were their father,' cleared the New Forest of its towns and villages for the same purpose.

(The 'Report of the Crofters' Commissioners' is, however, much more lenient to deer forests than was expected, and the following summary of their views on this point is extracted from the Report :—'The class of persons who find work in

---

[1] The average rent is 13*d.* per acre. Sheep runs pay only 10*d.* per acre.

connection with deer forests embrace masons, joiners, plas-
terers, plumbers, and slaters, with the labourers for each trade,
wire-fencers, road-makers, blacksmiths, carriers, besides local
shopkeepers and those actually employed during the shooting
season as gillies, with or without their ponies. It will be thus
seen that, contrary to what is probably the popular belief,
deer forests in a far greater degree than sheep farms afford
employment to the various classes above mentioned, and this
consideration forms, in our judgment, the most interesting of
all those which have been submitted to us. We have considered it our duty to record unequivocally the opinion that
the dedication of large areas exclusively to the purposes of
sport, as at present practised in the Highlands, does not
involve a substantial diminution of food-supply to the nation,
and we have amply recognised the various benefits which are
in many cases associated with the sporting system, where it is
exercised in a liberal and judicious spirit. In doing this our
design has been to qualify and correct erroneous impressions
which are prevalent in many quarters on this subject. We
would not, however, have it thought that the views which we
have here expressed imply an approval of the present appro-
priation of land in all cases to unproductive uses, far less an
undiscriminating application of additional tracts to a similar
purpose in future. It is our opinion that provisions should be
framed under which the crofting class would be protected
against any diminution, for the purpose of afforestment, of
arable or pasture area now in their possession, and by which
the areas which might hereafter form the most appropriate
scene for expanding cultivation, and small holdings, should be
preserved from curtailment; if this were done the interest of
the class for whom we are specially concerned would be effec-
tually secured.')
It is one of the most striking anomalies of our civilisation,
this surrendering back to a state of nature such vast tracts of
land in a country so densely populated as our own, and send-
ing forth such a steady stream of emigration to the remotest
parts of the world; and it is curious to remark that the
chase, the every-day enjoyment of the primitive savage, entirely reversing the general rule, becomes one of the costliest
luxuries by an advanced civilisation.
In the 'Report of the Commissioners of Inland Revenue'
(p. 182), we find that 57,700 licences to kill game were taken

out in 1884 ; [1] also 6,140 gamekeepers' licences, who have
under them a large staff of night-watchmen, &c., who do not
come under the tax. We also find that there are 21,000
sporting dogs for accompanying shooting and other sportsmen.
This luxury of the chase, pursued so enthusiastically by our
nobility and gentry, shows them to be possessed of a love of
healthy recreation, and a physical energy which it still further
develops, and is doubtless far more noble and manly than
those effeminate and voluptuous luxuries which have ever
marked the declining days of ancient civilisation ; but the
price paid for it is often out of all proportion with its results.

From the Report of the said Commissioners (28th Report,
p. 249), we find that in the year ended March 31, 1884, there
were 809,271 dwelling-houses, each of which paid a yearly
rental of over 20*l.*, the annual value of the whole being
42,098,442*l.* Eight pounds being the average rent of a workman's dwelling,[2] and thereby, according to the standard already fixed, representing the necessary in house accommodation, it follows that the annual luxurious expenditure in
houses is about 35,000,000*l.*

The balance of Schedule A is absorbed in about 18,000,000*l.*
for shops, farmhouses, &c., with a rental of 20*l.* and upwards,
and 37,000,000*l.* for houses under 20*l.* ; and about 25,000,000*l.*
for public messuages not charged.

Of the other items, casting out entirely the amount in
Schedule C, in respect of annuities, dividends, &c., as being
merely claims upon the resources of the nation, non-productive
of any return to it, and adding the remainder, including the
18,000,000*l.* for shops, warehouses, &c., the 70,000,000*l.* for
unreturned profits, the 40,000,000*l.* excused to incomes between 150*l.* and 400*l.*, and the 180,000,000*l.* not charged to
income tax (casting out about 50,000,000*l.* for interest upon
foreign loans along with Schedule C), we get a lump sum of
about 500,000,000*l.*, representing the annual value of capital,
other than lands, tenements, &c., and of the service of those,
other than the manual-labour classes, engaged in professions,
trades, employments, &c., which capital and service we may
fairly assume to be used for the benefit of all classes in the

[1] The Commissioners state that 'the evasion of this duty is very
general.'
[2] The average rental of all houses under 20*l.* in Great Britain is
about 8*l.* 1*s.* 6*d.*, there being in Great Britain 4,523,775 houses under
20*l.* with a rental of 36,519,654*l.*

proportion of their respective incomes, and of which the 750,000 families of the middle and upper classes, appropriating very nearly four-ninths, must expend luxuriously about 250,000,000*l.*

Stated briefly, then, the expenditure for the luxuries of wealth in capital and the services of the professional and commercial classes, and those other than the manual-labour classes, is estimated as follows :—

|  | £ |
|---|---|
| In respect of the luxurious occupation and application of the land . . . | 35,000,000 |
| In respect of the luxurious occupation of dwelling-houses . . . . . . | 35,000,000 |
| In respect of the luxurious application of railways, mines, ironworks, and all other capital except lands and tenements; also of the services of those, other than the working classes, engaged in professions, trades, employments, public offices, &c. . | 210,000,000 |
| In all . . . . . . . . . | 280,000,000 |

This, deducted from the total expenditure for the luxuries of wealth of 550,000,000*l.*, leaves 270,000,000*l.* as the sum which is paid over to the manual-labour classes for their work in producing and maintaining these luxuries. This is a sum greater by 10,000,000*l.* than that paid for all the rest of the labour of the working classes put together, and would seem to represent a proportionately greater number employed.

The average earning per worker in the United Kingdom is 42*l.* 10*s.*

In the table on the following page of various workers for luxury (keeping out the domestic servants) the average is 50*l.* ; but when they are included, it is reduced to 40*l.*, whilst the average of those employed in agriculture, in cotton, woollen, and linen, as weavers, dyers, and factory hands, as boot and shoe-makers, in mining and coal-mining, in the earthenware manufacture, and connected with iron and the other metals, as artisans and general labourers, on railways, and carriers by road and sea, in the army, navy, dockyards, Post Office, and police, by whom the great bulk of the necessaries are produced, the average is about 44*l.* 10*s.* per worker.

It may very safely be stated, therefore, that at least the complete half of our industrial population labours solely and exclusively for the luxuries of wealth.

Foremost and most conspicuous in the ranks of those who

minister to this luxury stand the domestic servants, numbering, as has been already stated, 1,951,000, with an income of
68,500,000*l.*, who are supplemented by a contingent of 288,000,
other services (taking two-thirds of the whole), paid at the
rate of 11,570,000*l.* As has been said before, it is impossible
to classify all our workers accurately as working either for
luxury or necessary ; but the following may be taken as an
approximation to the numbers of various workers for luxury :—

| | Persons | Wages £ |
|---|---|---|
| Domestic Servants (the whole) . . | 1,951,000 | 68,500,000 |
| Other Services (two-thirds) . . . | 288,000 | 11,570,000 |
| Builders (eleven-twentieths) . '. . | 404,000 | 23,000,000 |
| Cabinet-makers and French Polishers (two-thirds) . . . . . | 52,000 | 3,060,000 |
| Coachmakers and Saddlers (two-thirds). | 65,000 | 2,790,000 |
| Wood Carvers and Gilders (the whole) . | 19,000 | 1,490,000 |
| ¹Silk Manufacturers (two-thirds) . . | 40,000 | 1,360,000 |
| Hosiery, Glove and Button Manufac- turers (two-thirds) . . . . . . . . | 42,000 | 1,580,000 |
| Hair Wig Makers (two-thirds) . . | 11,000 | 860,000 |
| Goldsmiths and Lapidaries (nine- tenths) . . . . . . | 28,000 | 1,690,000 |
| | 2,900,000 | 115,900,000 |
| Workers of all other classes . . . | 3,230,000 | 154,100,000 |
| Total Workers for the Luxuries of Wealth . . . . . . | 6,130,000 | £ 270,000,000 |

Observe here how that the rich cannot consume their
possessions by themselves, but must share them amongst all
those who serve them ; whilst, on the other hand, those who
thus serve must in return exercise and exert their faculties
very beneficially for themselves.

And, fortunately, the striking inequality in the possession
of property is often more nominal than real ; for, as the wise
man says :—' When goods increase, they are increased that
eat them : and what good is there to the owners thereof, saving the beholding of them with their eyes?'² Things really
belong to those who use them, whoever may be the nominal
proprietors. The coachman is often the real owner of the
horses, the trainer of the racing stud, the crew of the pleasure
yacht, the workmen of the factory, and the servants of many

¹ Britain uses above half as much silk as the whole of the rest of
Europe.
² Eccles. v. 11.

of the finest mansions and pleasure-grounds in the country, the
.egal owners being often little more than signers of certain
documents in connection with their property ; whilst in every
case, by the beneficent constitution of things, the workers have
a certain unalienable co-proprietary right to the materials
which they are using.

In looking at these calculations, it must be carefully borne
in mind that all this expenditure of labour is solely and
entirely for luxury, and that the remaining half of the industrial population (aided by that portion of the professional,
commercial, tradesmen, and public official classes whose labour,
like their own, is for necessaries) not only support themselves,
but the whole of their fellows who minister both to wealthy
luxury and also to popular luxuriousness, which will hereafter
be discussed, and supply besides all that part of the maintenance of the 750,000 families, their superiors, which may be
fairly termed necessary; in short, that the labour of over six
millions of our industrial population supports themselves, the
other half who are thus free to minister exclusively to luxury,
and supplies to the upper classes all necessaries, so called.. To
sum up, the luxuriousness of wealth yearly appropriates for
its sole behoof the pleasant places of the land and their fruits;
the princely habitations which it has caused to be reared
thereon, with all their splendid and glittering appurtenances;
the produce of mines, ironworks, railways, &c., and the services
of the professional and commercial classes, to an extent represented by the vast sum of 280,000,000l.; and exacts as its right
the entire labour and homage of over six millions of manual
labourers, who, with their families, constitute over 13,000,000
of the population, at an expense of about 270,000,000l. ; while
out of the upper classes who monopolise all this wealth and
service only about 240,000 appear in the ' Report of the Inland
Revenue Commissioners' as rendering services in return in
the shape of professions, trades, employments, &c.; to which,
if there be added 60,000 for those engaged in public offices, &c.,
we have a total of only 300,000—merely two-fifths—who can
be set down as productive workers ; while the remaining
three-fifths, numbering 450,000 families, whom Mr. Dudley
Baxter terms the 'butterflies of fashion, so completely the
creatures of idleness, and who represent the most important (?)
of all the elements of production, the element of capital,'
enjoy their living [1] and luxuries entirely independent of any

[1] See Note 4 in Appendix to ' Luxury.'

E

service to the community which supports them. Of this
luxury nearly a half is appropriated by 650,000 families with
incomes under 1,000*l*., little less than a fourth by 90,000
families with incomes under 5,000*l*., and a little more than a
fourth by the upper ten thousand.

The pleasure navy of Britain in 1886 numbered, according
to Lloyd's, 2,767 registered yachts of all denominations, of
126,293 tons register, requiring about 11,500 hands to man
them, and representing an expenditure of about 3¼ millions
sterling.[1]

In the ' Report of the Commissioners of Inland Revenue '
we find that the following were charged to assessed taxes in
Great Britain in the year ended March 31, 1884 :—185,212
male servants, 470,285 carriages, and 57,081 armorial bearings.
In 1868 there were 337,462 horses used for pleasure and 2,532
race horses according to the Inland Revenue Returns.

These items are not now given, but must be considerably
increased.[2]

These are items and indications of a luxuriousness so vast,
compared with that which exists in any other European
country, that it strongly impresses intelligent foreigners [3] at the
first view of the residences of the wealthy portion of London
(the great centre to which flows the already concentrated
wealth of the United Kingdom), and of the dazzling magnificence of the spectacle presented by their gorgeous equipages
in its fashionable streets during ' the season.'

The extent to which the wealth of the country is concentrated in London may be partly realised from the fact that
whilst, notwithstanding the enormous amount of poverty-
stricken and consequently wretchedly housed people in the
metropolis, its house property per inhabitant averages 158*l*.,
that of the Provinces is 66*l*., of Scotland 60*l*., and of Ireland
only 12*l*.

A very great deal of the strife between labour and capital
has its origin deep seated in the withdrawal of the profits of

[1] The increase of yachting in Great Britain in thirty years has been
as follows :—

| Year | Clubs | Yachts | Year | Clubs | Yachts |
|------|-------|--------|------|-------|--------|
| 1853 | 18 | 1,046 | 1873 | 40 | 2,805 |
| 1863 | 18 | 1,348 | 1883 | 55 | 40,30 |

—Mulhall's *Dictionary of Statistics*.

See Note 5 in Appendix to ' Luxury.'
[2] See Note 6 in Appendix to ' Luxury.'
[3] See Note 7 in Appendix to ' Luxury.'

capital from their source, and their expenditure in the wealthy luxuriousness of our great cities, and especially of our metropolis.

The rent of land especially has hitherto been so easily collected, and the management of landed property has been so conveniently delegated to factor or bailiff, that this class of capitalist has been the foremost and most conspicuous in this gigantic centralising movement.

If a larger share of the profits realised by capital invested in our manufacturing industries were judiciously expended in connection with the industrial communities whose labours help to make them, there would be fewer strikes, and a more amicable intercourse between owners of works and workers all round, and it may be still more forcibly stated that, if a large portion of the rent of land were spent upon the land which yields it, there would be fewer No-rent manifestoes, and a more cordial relationship between landlord and tenant in every respect.

Without for one moment seeking to justify the lawless conduct of the Irish or Scottish tenants who, influenced by the teaching of socialistic agitators, have sought to resist the payment of rent altogether, it cannot be doubted that the luxurious expenditure of their rents by absentee landlords in our great metropolis, and in every capital in Europe, has been a powerful means of fanning the flames of discontent which have of late been spreading with such alarming violence.

This country, being not only a great commercial emporium like the ancient Tyre and Carthage, or the more modern Venice, but the greatest manufacturing nation that has ever existed, its wealthy hierarchy of 750,000 families, with the labour of the hardest working of all populations (controlled by more subtle knowledge and wider use of the vast material forces) at their entire disposal, possesses a power over the resources of all foreign lands entirely unexampled by the most luxurious of the ancient civilisations. Their gigantic luxuriousness not only marshals in the ranks of its mighty army craftsmen of every craft—artists of the cunning hand and labourers with stolid sinew—who, with a will and such aid as no other workers have ever had, labour at home, many of them dismally and drearily, from day to day and from year to year in its service; but it has made every other country one of its outposts, submitting to our conquering industry and yielding costly tribute.

For it the huntsman toils under the burning sun of Africa, perilling life and limb to supply the tusked ivory, gorgeous plumes, and variegated skins, and sledges under the biting cold of Canadian or Siberian winters for the glossy furs in which it wraps itself—for it the dusky Indian spends his short amphibious life in the pearl fishery, or digs, confined in sepulchral mines, for the gems with which it is bedecked—the sunny plains of France ring with the vintage shouts of those who produce its choicest banquet liquors—the mighty Ganges sweeps down its silk and spices to the great highway of the ocean, and the Niger carries 'its ivory, myrrh, and frankincense.' The sails of its merchantmen sweep round every coast, and remotest highway and desert resound with the noise of its traffickers ; and every land, and every river, and every isle of the sea contributes its quota to the costly store from which it daintily makes selection.

The inevitable dark background to this picture is the extreme poverty and destitution of vast numbers, even amongst the industrial classes, whose living is fearfully below the standard of even bare necessaries. If foreigners are impressed by the wealth and magnificence which they behold when they visit this country, they are no less astonished at the equally unparalleled squalor and misery which exist side by side with it.

The Commissioners appointed to inquire into the agricultural employment of women and children in England report that, in Dorset, the rate of wages to an able-bodied labourer, on the average, is rather less than ten shillings per week, including every perquisite in the shape of extra food, beer money, firing, and extra pay at hay-time and harvest. Out of this one-sixth has to be paid for rent of house, and it is only by feeding on coarse bread, potatoes, cabbage, and rice in scant allowance, with occasionally a bit of pork, that he can contrive to keep himself, wife, and two or three children in life.

And in a few of the other southern counties in England the same low rate of remuneration prevails.

The strike of the Warwickshire labourers has disclosed a state of things very little better in their county, whilst in many parts of Ireland it is much worse. Indeed, the condition of the whole class throughout the country is abject and mean in the extreme ; and vast hordes of our industrial population, engaged in labouring and mechanical pursuits in our towns and cities, though they may have a more liberal dietary, yet are so horribly cooped up, so continually breathe foul air in the workshop and fouler in their own dwellings, that their lot is not at all superior to that of the agricultural labourer. The inevitable retrogression (as well as progression) which has hitherto attended civilisation has been far too little accounted of. The prime necessaries of air, light, and space, enjoyed by the most primitive communities, are, in its great centres, the costliest luxuries ; and it is to the recovery of these vital necessaries for the use of our towns' labourers and artisans, more than to their progress in artificial refinement, that social reformers should, in the meantime, devote all their energy.

## POPULAR LUXURIES.

But turn to the other side of the case. The counterpart of this luxuriousness, that moral condition of society which encourages abnormal accumulation of wealth by the few, is the unfitness of the many for the use of larger means of life than the residuum left by their wealthier fellows—often men of much the same moral calibre as themselves.

> Ill fares the land, to hastening ills a prey,
> Where wealth accumulates and men decay,

the decay of the men being often more the cause than the result of the accumulation. The luxuriousness of the wealthy part of our population (by which thousands of them are yearly gravitating downwards into the very lowest strata of society) only has been discussed ; I now desire to hold up to comparison with it, and to demonstrate as one of its great causes, the luxuriousness of the working classes themselves. They are more thoroughly luxurious in the expenditure of their means than their superiors, and are joint supporters with them of many of the most objectionable luxuries—the sensational dramas, burlesques, and obscene dances of the stage, the excitement and gambling of the racecourse, and vicious amusements which it is not necessary here to mention.[1]

Within the last century the diet of the people has undergone a complete revolution, and the use of the luxuries of tea and coffee has 'become almost a second nature with both sexes and every class of our countrymen.' The conviction is now spreading more and more widely that this 'sloppy diet,'

[1] See Note 8 in Appendix to ' Luxury.'

as Cobbett calls it, is entirely inferior in nutriment to the
simple fare of former days, and that from its stimulating
effects has arisen much of the nervous and dyspeptic complaints
so characteristic of the present generation.

With many factory operatives it is tea (and very often that
abominable decoction, boiled tea) to breakfast, tea to dinner,
and tea to supper, especially amongst the females, and so much
impressed with the evils attendant upon this luxurious form
of diet, have been the Firm of which the Writer is a partner,
that they have provided the means for their workers obtaining
the more solid and nutritious articles of diet at a little less
than cost price, and with capital results.

The enormous proportion of rickety children—that is,
children with legs too weak to carry their bodies—in Glasgow
has become so alarming that it has excited the attention of
the medical faculty in a marked degree ; and their conclusion
is that the substitution of tea and sugar for milk and oatmeal
has been the main cause of it.  In one district in the neighbourhood of Glasgow, it was found that as much as twenty
tons of sugar were used for one of oatmeal.

To quote from Mr. Dudley Baxter's work on the ' Taxation
of the United Kingdom,' pp. 69–77 ; and from Professor
Levi's work on the ' Wages and Earnings of the Working
Classes,' p. 60.  ' The consumption of TEA has increased from
880,000 lbs. in 1741 to 111,000,000 lbs. in 1867, and to
180,000,000 lbs. in 1884 ; and COFFEE from 130,000 lbs. in 1740
to 31,300,000 lbs. in 1867, and 35,000,000 lbs. in 1884.[1]  Every
individual of the working classes now consumes, on the average,
4¾ pounds of tea during the year, in the place of one in 1841,
and of 1½ in 1857.  The consumption in middle higher class
families is at the rate of 6 lbs. per member.  Every child of a
working-class family now gets, on the average, twice as much
sugar as in 1857, to supply the deficiency of a scanty diet.'
The consumption of sugar has increased from 15 lbs. per
inhabitant in 1840 to 70 lbs. in 1884.

The consumption of TOBACCO (Mulhall, p. 449) has increased
from 10,900,000 lbs. in 1789 to 40,800,000 lbs. in 1867, and
to 52,000,000 lbs. in 1884.  The taxation voluntarily paid by
the 6,500,000 adult males of the working classes for its consumption amounts to an average poll tax of 19s. each.  This
represents 5½ lbs. a year, or 1¾ oz. per week, which is considered

---

[1] The consumption of coffee has declined a little within the last
twenty years.

a moderate family allowance. The amount varies from 1 oz. a week with the agricultural labourer or poor mechanic, up to 4 or even 6 oz. a week with constant smokers among the well-paid artisans. In some places, as at Sheffield, the wives frequently share their husbands' tobacco, and smoke from 2 to 3 oz. per week. I am told that about three-fourths of the working-men smoke, and that 2 oz. per week is the commonest scale of consumption.' The total value of tea and coffee as sold to private consumers in 1884 is estimated at 18,300,000*l.*, and of tobacco at 13,100,000*l.*

ALCOHOL, however, is the most gigantic and prominent of the POPULAR LUXURIES. That there are more people connected with the liquor trade than with our three greatest and most vaunted manufacturing industries, and more capital invested in it than in any two of them, are the startling results at which Mr. Leone Levi, writing in 1870, arrives by careful and well-founded investigations. He calculates that there are upwards of 150,000 licensed houses, and assumes that four persons are employed in each. He sets down 100,000 as engaged in bottling and coopering, 66,000 in malting and brewing, almost an equal number in the cultivation of barley, 12,000 in the production of hops, 6,000 in distilling and recti-fying, and 2,000 in bottle and cork-making, giving the aston-ishing total of 846,000 persons directly engaged in the liquor traffic ; and, counting those dependent on them, of 1,500,000 persons interested in it. It is only possible to realise to some extent the magnitude of these figures by contrast. According to the factory returns of 1869, 401,000 persons were employed in cotton mills, 118,000 in woollen mills, and 160,000 in iron-works, in all 679,000 ; or, with those dependent on them added, 1,200,000. The capital invested in the making and selling of liquors is estimated at 117,100,000*l.*, in the cotton trade at 85,500,000*l.*, in the woollen trade at 22,600,000*l.*, and in the iron trade at 25,500,000*l.*

Quoting from Mr. Hoyle, himself a large employer of labour (' Our National Resources, and How they are Wasted ') :— ' During the four years ending 1869, the annual average ex-penditure upon intoxicating drinks was 112,590,550*l.* In four years we spent upon intoxicating drinks 450,398,201*l.* ; and yet upon cotton goods, during the same period, we spent (reckoning ten per cent. for retailers' profits) only 51,625,842*l.*'

According to another calculation, an amount of grain equal to the whole produce of Scotland, reserving only seed for

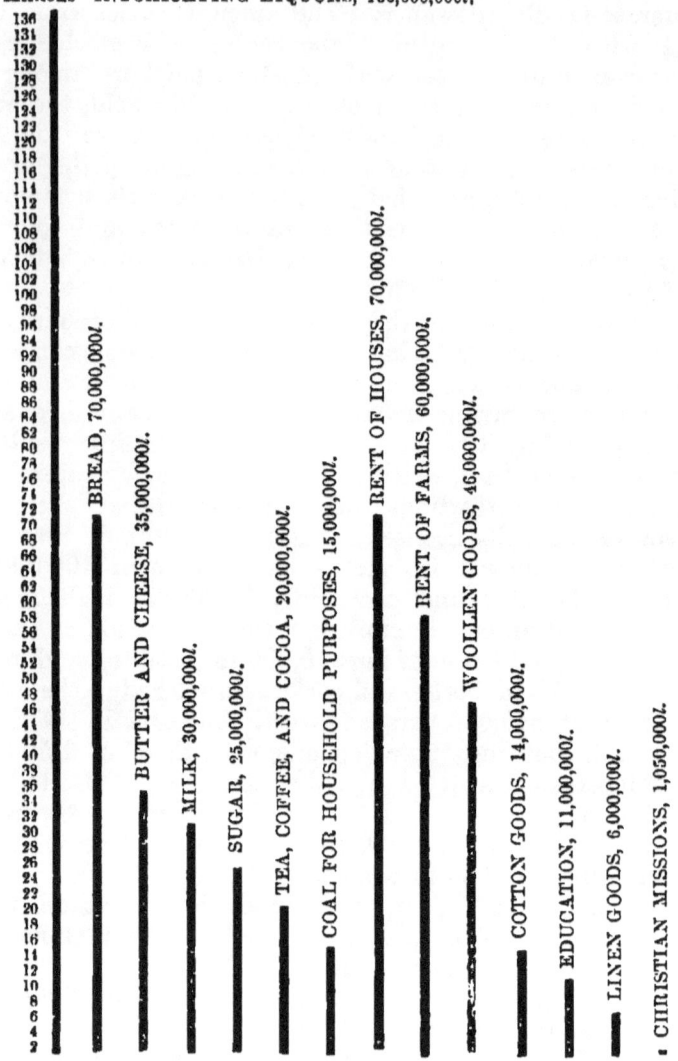

*How we Spend our Money.*

1st. The money spent upon intoxicating liquors in the United Kingdom is nearly twice as great as the total amount paid for BREAD.

2nd. We pay nearly four times as much for intoxicating liquors as we pay for BUTTER and CHEESE.

3rd. We spend four and a half times as much upon drink as we spend upon MILK.

another year, is annually consumed in the manufacture of this drink, thus involving a waste of land beside which that of the deer forests sinks into comparative insignificance. And Mr. Hoyle goes on to say (p. 98) :—' Under any circumstances we shall be considerably within the mark in assuming that the direct and indirect cost to the nation, arising from the use of intoxicating liquors, cannot be less than 200,000,000*l.* yearly.'

The figure given by Mr. Hoyle (who, I am sorry to say, has recently gone over to the great majority) for the drink is 126,349,256*l.*

The admirable table on page 56, constructed by Joseph Spencer, from figures by William Hoyle, and published by the United Kingdom Alliance, shows the annual expenditure of the United Kingdom on intoxicating liquors, compared with various other of the chief items of expenditure in daily life, for the ten years ending 1882.

It is calculated that the proportion consumed by the working classes is a little more than two-thirds of the whole, and that of the 36*s.* per week or 93*l.* per annum which constitutes their average income, they expend about at least 20*l.* on luxuries, more than one-fifth of their income, and of this 20*l.*, about 17*l.* 10*s.* is for drink and tobacco alone, including the taxes thereon, whilst their average expenditure for house rent is only 8*l.*

The supporters of the Malthusian doctrine, like the phrenologists at first, who looked entirely to the phenomena connected with the brain only, and entirely overlooked the potent influences exercised upon it by the correlated organs, so potent

---

4th. We spend more than five times as much upon drink as we do upon Sugar, and nearly seven times as much as all our expenditure upon Tea, Coffee, and Cocoa.

5th. We spend more upon drink than the Rent Roll of all the Farms and all the Houses in the United Kingdom.

6th. We spend about twice as much upon drink as our total expenditure upon Woollen, Cotton, and Linen.

7th. Beside the enormous expenditure upon drink, we have to pay poor and police rates, costs of Insanity, Crime, Vagrancy, Accidents, Disease, loss of labour, premature death, &c., giving at the very least another 100,000,000*l.*, and making a total loss to the nation of more than 200,000,000*l.* yearly.

WORKING MEN ! This is the way the money goes ! and the reason why trade is so bad ! If you want to be prosperous, avoid drink and shun the public-house.

as generally to stultify their most careful calculations, have
not taken into account, amongst other important modifying
causes, the pressure of luxuriousness (as well as of population)
on the means of subsistence. In addition to the immense
field opened up by emigration to new countries for obeying the
Divine command to 'increase and multiply and replenish the
earth,' there would, in the older and more densely populated,
be no less scope afforded by restriction of the use of injurious
luxuries. Their abolition in our own country would allow of
an increase of population to be reckoned by the tens of millions, and with a higher standard of living than at present.

The total taxes on stimulants in the United Kingdom are
42,900,000*l.* They form about five-eighths of the imperial
taxation and two-fifths of the total taxation, both imperial and
local, of the United Kingdom. Of this total, tea, coffee, &c.,
amount to 5,700,000*l.*, while alcoholic liquors and tobacco
amount to 37,200,000*l.* The latter is therefore an income tax,
paid in hard cash to the Treasury through the medium of the
retailer, of nearly 7*d.* in the pound on the gross income of
every man, woman, and child in the United Kingdom, or a
poll tax of more than a pound. The whole of the imperial
taxation of the working classes is on their luxuries, the main
weight being on their alcohol and tobacco ; it amounts to about
26*s.* per head, whilst the local taxes are only about 10*s.* more.

In fact, now the British workman does not pay one far-
thing of imperial taxes except on his luxuries, and this should
always be particularly noted.

Mr. Henry George puts his panacea 'into practical form
by proposing ('Progress and Poverty,' p. 288) to abolish all
taxation save that upon land values,' but no juster or more
beneficial taxation could be devised than this upon luxuries,
which conserves for national purposes a great portion of their
waste, and, especially in the case of alcohol, limits the spread
of intemperance by making it more costly. The United
Kingdom is, with the exception of Scandinavia, the lightest
taxed of European States.

The manner in which British taxation has been reduced,
whilst that of all other European countries has been increased,
is thus stated in an article in the 'Leisure Hour' :—'In 1826,
ten years after the great wars, although taxes had been reduced in the interval, the amount of taxation raised in the
United Kingdom was 55,825,000*l.* ; in 1851, just before the
Crimean War, the amount was 54,485,000*l.* ; now the amount

is 68,514,000*l*. Instead of doubling, as it might have done, had it increased proportionately to our numbers, or quadrupling to our wealth, the amount levied in taxation has only been added to one-fourth part as compared with what it was half a century ago. Per head, in spite of our increase in wealth, it is only 41*s*. 5*d*. now against 49*s*. 5*d*. in 1826. There is thus a wide margin for our Chancellors of the Exchequer, even if they should not seek to go beyond raising the sum of two hundred millions, which even now might be raised, merely keeping the proportions to numbers which existed sixty years ago, and making no allowance whatever for the intermediate increase of wealth. So far, therefore, from indulging in national extravagance as our wealth has increased, we have kept far within bounds, and there is a huge margin to come and go upon before we even begin to lay upon shoulders more able to bear them burdens like those which were borne sixty years ago. Curiously enough, England stands alone among European States in this diminution of national burdens. The taxation of France in the same period has increased from 20*s*. 1*d*. to 43*s*. 7*d*. per head, and in Prussia, Belgium, Russia, and Holland, there has equally been an increase per head.' [1]

The statistics of the liquor trade, previously given, correspond with the general conviction that an enormous number of the working classes ' waste their substance and destroy their health in this, the most insidious of all social luxuries.' As Mr. Baxter wrote in his work on ' Taxation ' :—

' The gin-palace allures its throng of monomaniacs. The Custom House officer takes toll at the door. The Excise officer stands beside the till, and seizes nearly half the price of every glass that is poured. Emaciated and in rags, the drunkard puts down the wages that should have supported his children, calling for glass after glass until his earnings are exhausted, and then staggers off to a poverty-stricken home to wreak his madness on his wife. Thousands and tens of thousands are merely funnels for drink, and divide all the sweat of their brow between the distiller and the State. Out of their folly the nation draws more than six millions of money, a twelfth of her whole revenue, sufficient to support half her navy, nearly sufficient to feed her destitute poor.

And it is not merely the injury which this debased morality works upon its special victims which must be taken into

¹ See Note 9 in Appendix to ' Luxury.'

account, but also its pernicious effects upon all connected
with them. It lowers the general standard of living, for the
drunkard will house, or rather hovel, himself like a pig [1] ; it reduces the remuneration of labour, for he is obliged to sell his
work for the lowest pittance, and his progeny, at the earliest
age, swell the ranks of the drudges of the labour market ; he
forfeits all respect by his abject, cringing servility for the sake
of even a momentary gratification of his passion ; and in all
this the good men and true, who are bound up with him ' in
the bundle of life '—the honest, steady, temperate workmen,
the work of whose hands it is which really produces our vast
material resources—are dragged down with him ; while the
capitalist, who has to control him, must of necessity treat all
the class to which he belongs with the rigour due to him
alone ; and he has taught the wealthy idle, into whose hands
his utter wastefulness has caused so much property to concen-
trate, to look upon our working-men with haughty contempt
or supercilious indifference.

The writer knows of large workshops in Glasgow, the
types of vast numbers throughout the country, the workmen
in which can earn from 30s. to 80s. per week ; but so thoroughly addicted are they all to the vice of intemperance, that
their employers have to dole out their wages piecemeal ; they
are clothed in old and beggarly habiliments ; their families
are in that fearful state of abject poverty to be met with only
in our great centres of civilisation, and which must be seen to
have the slightest idea of, so completely from hand to mouth
that they would actually starve were the master to withhold
for a day the shilling or two of what is technically called
' subsist,' generally not to be entrusted into the hands of the
operative himself, but of one of his family who calls for it.
Tuesday at mid-day is the recognised time for beginning the
week's work, after the utter prostration caused by the Bacchanalian orgies of Saturday and Sunday. When sick they go
into the hospital as a matter of course, and have to be buried
at the expense of the parish or by subscription. So thoroughly
degraded is the moral tone of many of these workshops, that
no tool of any value can be used, as it would immediately find
its way to the pawnbroker. These workmen referred to are
engaged in some of the lighter and more luxurious branches
of manufacture ; but in almost all trades, rough or refined, we

[1] See Note 10 in Appendix to ' Luxury.'

find the same appalling state of affairs. Recent official investigations into the 'Employment of Brickyard Children in England' furnish a multitude of confirmatory evidence. Let one instance speak for thousands :—

'A girl, who began at nine years old to load for her father, had at thirteen a crooked ankle and a knee grown out at one side, the result of undue physical exertion. The man had three sons, the youngest only eight, at work with him, yet he actually kept his poor deformed daughter working like the rest, although the net wages of himself and children could not have been less than 4*l.* per week.' Your luxurious workman is a thorough savage in his fierce spells of work and prolonged fits of idleness after intemperate orgies ; and, like the savage also, to pamper his luxurious appetite he never scruples to enslave his wife and children. Our factory legislation had to rescue women and children as much from the oppression of their husbands and fathers as from that of their employers. 'The brickmakers, as a class, are among the most highly remunerated of English working people. During the six months which form the brick-making season a single workman and his family will earn from 140*l.* to 220*l.*, and yet, to use the expressive language of one of their own community, in winter they have "scarcely a crust of bread to eat or a stick of furniture to sit on." Everything goes in drink.'[1]

Some of our highest social science authorities, such as Mr. Recorder Hill, of Birmingham, and Lord Brougham, have been so much impressed with the magnitude of the evils of the drinking habits of the people, as to believe that nine-tenths of all the crime in the kingdom is caused by them. That it is allied with this proportion of crime may, at any rate, be safely affirmed. Drunkenness is the delusive refuge into which, in the Anglo-Saxon race especially, human nature, working below its proper healthy, moral, and consequently happy tone, almost inevitably rushes, and its prevalence may therefore be taken as a fair index of the general immorality.

As long as this vicious luxuriousness remains, to our working classes may still be addressed the spirit of the lofty words of Menenius Agrippa to the luxurious and degraded Roman populace :—

> I tell you, friends, most charitable care
> Have the patricians of you. For your wants,

---

[1] See Note 11 in Appendix to 'Luxury.'

Your suffering in this dearth, you may as well
Strike at the heaven with your staves as lift them
Against the Roman state.[1]

Not the burdens of dictatorial capital, not the pressure of
aristocratic magnificence, nor the maintenance of a gigantic
system of polished luxury, beside which that in ancient times
called regal or imperial would look paltry and economical, so
much as your own vicious luxuriousness confine you to

perpetual durance, a restraint,
Though all the world's vastidity you had—
To a determined scope.[2]

It has been written as 'with a pen of iron upon the rock
for ever,' that not in material, but altogether in moral, progress, shall the amelioration of the economic condition of the
people consist ; that only by righteousness can a nation be
exalted.   The higher wages which followed the introduction
of steam-power, and the countless mechanical inventions which
turned it to account, in Lancashire especially, where it has
been most taken advantage of, instead of enriching, strength-
ening, and educating, in the ignorant and immoral hands of
the workmen, positively helped to make them poorer, feebler
more sensual and ignorant ; and well was it for the nation,
themselves included, that the superior men amongst them
were, partly by this very improvidence and ignorance, raised
into such a position of power as capitalists that they could
take from them, with the strong and stern hand, that which,
while being wasted, would have wasted their own souls, and,
though devoting it generally to the maintenance of a huge
system of refined luxury, rescue it from the tenfold worse
abuse of gluttony, debauchery, and idleness.   Better far that
labour be applied to rear the gorgeous palace and sculptured
monument, to fabricate purple and fine linen, to fashion the
equipages and supply the menials of a costly pageantry, than
be squandered in the sensual and degraded amusements of a
vicious populace.

As surfeit is the father of much fast,
So every scope by the immoderate use
Turns to restraint.[3]

That popular luxuriousness, the result of enfeebled morality
and inseparably allied with cognate vices, is a great cause of

[1] *Coriolanus*, act i. scene 1.        [2] *Measure for Measure.*
[3] *Ibid.*

concentration of property into few hands, may be laid down as a rule of that higher moral economy which dominates the so-called political, and which thus wrests from a people that which would but further degrade them, and conserves it for the maintenance of the higher and less injurious luxuries of the rich—not its noblest use, certainly, but the best possible under the circumstances. Just as the want of self-restraint and incapability for self-government in a nation raise up by stern moral necessity the military dictator, so do the luxurious indulgence and consequent immorality of an industrial population necessitate the rule of that great commercial dictator, the capitalist. The new modes of manufacturing industry caused by the introduction of steam machinery, and requiring the combination of thousands of workers, not far enough advanced in intelligence, sobriety, and honesty to combine themselves, raised by a powerful moral and economical necessity the great British capitalists, generally from the very ranks of the working classes themselves. The landed estate has always been the great object to which the ambition of wealthy manufacturers and merchants has aspired, and thus a centralisation in the possession of the land, to the greater extent already stated, followed as a natural result of the centralisation of capital. Besides, land had increased in value to such an enormous extent with the increase of manufacturers, especially land with mineral resources, and in and around the great manufacturing centres, that its large hereditary owners were placed in a position to add vastly to their patrimonies. Had the small landowners, however, been equal to the spirit of the time, no power on earth could have wrenched from them their property ; but the increased luxuriousness and improvidence of their habits caused the almost total surrender of their small freeholds at the immensely higher prices to which the new order of things had raised them. In Scotland especially the drunkenness (the prominent social vice of the class and period), and consequent laziness, improvidence, and imbecility of the 'wee lairds' of the last century caused the beneficial system of small lairdships, which, under frugal and industrious management, had reared such a splendid yeomanry, the very backbone and pride of the nation, to collapse at once before the mighty energy of this new development of manufacturing industry.

When increased dominion over the material world is obtained, so that fewer men can perform the same work, either

by the slow processes which in ancient times paved the way of
civilisation, or suddenly, as of late, by the giant aid of steam
and its contemporaries, there are two ways in which the
greater number of supernumeraries may be employed. If the
morality of the people thus superiorly endowed expand in har-
mony with their enlarged means, then their higher tastes and
capacities so elevate the level of their economic condition, and
demand so many luxuries as necessaries, that the bulk of the
increased power is expended in the production of these higher
necessaries in the service of the many, and the smaller part is
appropriated by luxury, which maintains its relative position
in advance, and the proper balance is duly preserved ; but if
morality retrograde, or if it even stand still, then the most of
the gain is for luxuriousness—the surplus workmen are devoted
to the service of the few. And it has been their entire overlooking of this great truth, their utter aversion to the recog-
nition of the supremacy of moral over all material causes in
the progress of society, which have stultified so many treatises
of the political economists.

The words of the Master are :—' Seek ye first the Kingdom
of God and his righteousness, and all these things shall be
added unto you ; ' and in the wake of all the great moral
reformers, though nobly unconscious of other than spiritual
fruit to their work, there most assuredly has followed, as a
secondary result, the elevation of the social and economical
condition of the people. Providence seldom confers larger
powers without enlarging the capacity to use them ; man is
generally trained for the instruments which are put into his
hands. Contemporary with Watt, and Hargreaves, and
Crompton, Bell and the Stephensons, men of great spiritual
power were at work—the Wesleys, Wilberforce, Howard,
Chalmers, and a host of others—men of burning zeal and
ardent soul, who permeated the intelligence of the time with
the spirit of Heaven, and so guided the flood of inventive and
constructive genius that, instead of rushing on with swollen
fury, working havoc in its course, it gently expended many
beneficent results over the wide surface of society at large.
The abolition of slavery in our dominions, at great money loss
to ourselves, however injudiciously carried out, was one of the
noblest acts of political morality on record, and the evidence
of a lofty national rectitude of conduct which has insured the
right and proper use of a vast amount of our increased means,
and secured all of progress (and there has been much) which

has marked the social and economic condition of our working classes during the past century.

So vast, however, were the results of the application of steam-power, that it must be admitted the capacity to use them aright did not keep pace with their growth. Men in legions, whose services had been most necessary to the community, suddenly found themselves supplanted by machines, and reduced to a state of idleness, while production increased faster than the people could wisely make use of the products. Mr. Hoyle calculates ('Our National Resources, and How they are Wasted,' p. 5) 'that one individual, aided by the machinery of the present day, will produce as much yarn as 750 persons could have done little over one hundred years ago ;' and this is quoted here as merely one instance of that enormous industrial progress, the extent of which has been more particularly recounted in the preceding chapters on ' Labour ' and ' Leisure.'

A phase of civilisation never before witnessed was presented by this sudden and peaceful acquisition of a labour power equal to the united strength of about seventy million men. The old conquering races, when by the sword they compelled whole nations to slavery, furnish the only examples at all analogous. The nation found itself suddenly enriched by this conquest over the material world to a degree which renders insignificant the richest spoils of war brought into their territories by the greatest military conquerors of ancient or modern times ; but it found itself also very much in the position of a profligate who has unexpectedly come into a fortune, of a vulgar *parvenu* who does not know how to apply the service placed at his command except to purposes of idle ostentation. The hundreds of thousands of the agricultural labourers, already mentioned as having been rendered supernumerary by improvements in agriculture, and other means much more objectionable, and the still greater numbers of the manufacturing population supplanted by machinery, instead of going to swell the army of productive workmen, and advance the standard of living for all, were, many of them, transferred into the service of a vicious popular luxuriousness, but vastly more to minister to the luxuries of wealth. The distillery, the beershop, the tobacco trade, the low theatre and music saloon, and the poor's house, supported by the higher wages of the working classes on the one hand, and the countless luxuries demanded by the immensely greater and more concentrated wealth, indirectly resulting from this vicious luxuriousness on

F

the other, absorbed this gain of labour in the manner and to the extent already shown.

But along with the excess came the countercheck. The tremendous Continental war, at the end of the last and beginning of the present century, drafted into its serried ranks thousands and tens of thousands of the supernumerary population before increasing luxuriousness had time to appropriate their services, and so taxed our vastly increased material resources as to render necessary the frugal and temperate use of them. Historians see in the introduction of steam machinery, and especially in the inventions connected with the cotton manufacture, the preparing of gigantic sinews of war, wherewith successfully to combat a military despotism of unparalleled power and ambition ; but I am not aware that any have pointed out the equal counter-necessity for that severe drain upon our resources, both of men and material, caused by the French war—that heavy weight upon the other end of the beam whereby the Omnipotent—who sees the necessity for creating not only ' the smith that bloweth the coals in the fire, and that bringeth forth an instrument for his work, but also the waster to destroy ' [1]—maintained the equipose. No other part of recent history can better

> manifest eternal providence,
> And justify the way of God to men.

In countless instances, in the desolate, blackened track of war has sprung up the sweet, green herbage of a simpler life, where before flourished the growth of rank luxuriousness.

But are there no other means save the inexorable scourge of war or destitution wherewith to combat this dire evil ? is there no way of eliminating the tares from the fine wheat but by the cutting down of both ? must poverty and pauperism always keep pace with the increase of wealth ? Luxuriousness, proportionate to the centralisation of their wealth, has been the phenomenon witnessed by the civilisations of all ages, and has baffled the power of the most vigorous governments and laughed at all sumptuary enactments.

The whole aim of Mr. Henry George's celebrated work on ' Progress and Poverty' is to prove that ' the remedy for the unjust and unequal distribution of wealth apparent in modern civilisation, and for all the evils which flow from it,' lies in that modified form of communism which would ' substitute for the

[1] Isaiah liv. 16.

individual ownership of land a common ownership ' (' Progress
and Poverty,' p. 233). 'Nothing else' (he says) 'will go to
the cause of the evil—in nothing else is there the slightest
hope.
'This, then, is the true remedy for the unjust and unequal
distribution of wealth apparent in modern civilisation, and for
all the evils which flow from it : we must make land common
property.'

Entirely overlooking the great dominating moral factors in
this most difficult social problem, which I have attempted to
elucidate in this chapter, he asserts with a presumption and
easy assurance, which are marvellous in one who has shown so
much astuteness in discussing some other subjects of political
economy, that all the evils arising from inequality in the possession of property, and which I have shown to have their
origin and existence in causes deep down in the very constitution of human nature and its moral conditions, can be abolished
by a single, simple legislative enactment.

'What I, therefore, propose' (he says, 'Progress and
Poverty,' p. 288) 'as the simple, yet sovereign, remedy which
will raise wages, increase the earnings of capital, extirpate
pauperism, abolish poverty, give remunerative employment to
whoever wishes it, afford free scope to human powers, lessen
crime, elevate morals and taste and intelligence, purify government, and carry civilisation to yet nobler heights, is to appropriate rent by taxation.'

The spread of communistic ideas amongst our working
classes, which is likely to be the case from the perusal of such
clever special pleading as Mr. George's, especially as his book
has met with large support from many of the better classes,
and, above all, the belief in the pernicious political doctrine
that their improvement is to be effected by government
measures, and entirely outside of their own efforts, as is so
much the case amongst French workmen, would have the most
disastrous effect upon their future, and one of the objects in
republishing this chapter on 'Luxury,' and as part of a treatise
on our practical political economy, is to warn the people
against such false teaching, and show them that the path of
true progress lies almost entirely in the amelioration of their
own moral condition.

With miserly, mole-like instincts, the Political Economist
preaches increased production (and, for the attainment of this
end, the still greater increase and concentration of wealth in

the hands of the capitalists) as the great panacea of all poverty,
while the inexorable logic of facts has shown that, without
higher morality to guide increased wealth, it serves only to
heap higher the glittering but baneful pile of wealthy luxuries,
and sink into deeper sloughs the vicious popular luxuriousness
upon which this rears itself.

The Communist, thinking it to be a nefarious arrangement
of mere external force, ignorant of the moral, and consequently
eternal, impossibility of a vicious populace sharing alike,
instead of attacking the cause, wages war against all inequality
of property and luxury in any shape but that of the lowest
debauchery and idleness.

In England the communistic theory has always instinctively
been felt to be unnatural and impracticable,[1] and that a certain gradation in the modes of life (implying the moderate use
of luxuries by the superior classes) so stimulates, combines,
and directs industry as to afford to the working classes a more
liberal style of living, even though a large expenditure of their
labour is devoted to the production of luxuries, and to the rich
these luxuries into the bargain ; yet that the present standard
of living amongst our working classes should be very much
raised, and the luxuriousness of our wealthy classes very
much diminished, is the earnest desire of the wisest and best
writers on our social condition.   For the attainment of this
end the most diverse legislative schemes have been proposed ;
but all social reformers who do not penetrate to the great,
underlying, eternal, moral causes of the present condition of
society, have but a feeble and one-sided grasp of their subject.
The better informed of our political economists have of late
been more and more decidedly pointing to a 'moral remedy for
the mortifying mischief.'

'The indefinite control which the collective mind and
habit of society have over the element of population' is the
key-note of Chalmers's treatise ; honesty is the great cardinal
virtue upon which Mr. Ruskin makes all his schemes for the
amelioration of the condition of the masses to turn ; and temperance, enforced if necessary, is the panacea upheld by a large
number of living reformers.

But it is not upon any one virtue, important though it

---

[1] Even in such an interested assembly as the Trades' Union Congress,
on September 11, 1884, a motion 'that private property in land should
no more be tolerated than private property in the air we breathe,' was
lost by 50 votes to 35.

may be, that we must rely for improving the condition of the masses—not upon self-restraint alone, though it may do much —not upon honesty and temperance alone, though they may do more, but upon a general advance in the whole moral tone of society—such an advance as would entirely alter the present relationship between labour and capital, and develop a higher type of economic life.

The centralising power of capital has performed a grand and necessary work, in forming the present system of united labour. With giant sweep it has circled the lands, and drawn from his solitary bench the craftsman of every craft, and with iron hand put him into his place in the great workshop, assigning him his share of work to fit in with all other work, and disciplining him in the ranks of our army of workmen. But the proper countercheck to this vast, beneficial, centripetal, economic organisation, to make it work harmo niously and beneficently, has yet to be developed. Trades Unionism aims at becoming the great, centrifugal, economic power, and has, doubtless, served the purpose in a violent manner and limited degree. Counterchecks, however, do not work well in the line of direct resistance, but as exhibited in the great balancing powers of the universe. The extreme result of the struggle, as waged between Trades Unionist and Capitalist, was recently exhibited in the shipbuilding trade upon the Thames—the capital lying stagnant, the workmen starving, the trade driven to other localities—and in the glass bottle trade, which has been entirely driven out of the country. Trades Unionism, moreover, has this vital drawback, that much of the gain which it wrests from the luxuries of the rich goes to the support of a more degraded popular luxuriousness.

The new and rapidly expanding system of Co-operation, however, possesses all the requisites of a proper countercheck, and if the morality of the working classes be found sufficient for its proper development, it will satisfy one of the highest necessities of the time, and afford a splendid solution to the most vexed of all social questions. Its great beauty and fitness consists in this, that, while much more widely distributing the products of our labour, it carefully conserves that system of combination which has made this labour so successful. In its first or initiatory stage, the only one yet largely attained, and regarding which so much has been written and spoken as to make everyone familiar with its mode of working, the

operatives own and manage the shops which supply themselves with all the necessaries of life, and divide, or, better still,
save up for purposes of wider scope, the profits derived from
their business. Co-operation, in its highest development,
consists in the workmen possessing and combining all the
capital required for carrying on the several occupations in
which they are engaged, and, of course, dividing among them
the profits which now flow into the hands of the capitalists.
As to the possibility of the working classes being able to
acquire this capital, the money paid by them for drink and
tobacco alone could secure to them the whole of it employed in
trades, professions, occupations, &c., in ten years, and purchase all the land of the country in twenty years more ; and
let no one, with the brilliant examples of this system, inaugurated at Rochdale and practised in various other parts of the
kingdom besides, consider it Utopian and chimerical. Even
the more limited form of the ' co-operative principle, the basis
of which is the division of surplus profit between capital and
labour,' has been found to produce very beneficial results, and
is extending rapidly in many parts of the country.[1] The
highest form of co-operation, however, is only to be attained
by slow degrees, and after long and careful training in the
lower. The magnitude of the movement towards this goal is
so great that Mr. Hughes has ventured to say ' that it has
already done more than any other religious or social movement
of our day,' and a detailed account of it is given in a succeeding chapter ' On the Acquisition of Property by the Working
Classes.'

It is immensely better that wealth should be retained in
numerous moderate competencies than that it should vastly
accumulate in the hands of even superior men—even such
men as Mr. Peabody, who acted only as its liberal dispenser.
The reticent hundreds, each wisely seeing to the expenditure
of his own independent income, are necessarily far fitter to
make good use of means, and form a far nobler society, than
the eleemosynary crowd, with the wisest men in Christendom
for almoners. Indeed, the steady strain of luxury, appropriating just what is yielded by the ignorance, intemperance,
dishonesty, and consequent disunion of labour, is a very much
better thing for society, with its existing morality, as the
general rule, than would have been the laxness of an equally

[1] It has, however, since this was written, in many cases been
abandoned.

extensive and indiscriminate giving in charity. But the previous self-restraint, temperance, prudence, economy, intelligence, and honesty implied in the commencing and working
of co-operation, guarantee the proper use of the very much
larger share of the nation's resources to be derived through it
by the working classes.

We have seen what a vast number of the poor gain their
livelihood by ministering to the luxuries of the rich ; but there
has been no more preposterous and common fallacy than the
belief that the greater the consumption of luxuries the better
for industry, and that with the departure of luxuriousness the
working classes would lose half the source of their employment.
To provide themselves with the essential necessaries which
they now lack, to enable them to advance in intelligence,
refinement, and command of the elegances of life to the
position now occupied by many of the middle classes, would
require an amount of labour far exceeding that now expended
upon luxury. As Mr. Dudley Baxter wisely remarks ('Taxation of the United Kingdom,' pp. 47, 48) :—'Rich men are
not the only employers of labour. Every workman, in respect
of the articles that he consumes, is an employer of the pro-
ducer. A thousand workmen, each with 70*l.* a year of earnings,
are as large, and far more constant an employer than a single
millionaire, with 70,000*l.* a year income.'

And when the thousand workmen shall have progressed,
by their self-restraint, temperance, and frugality, to such a
position that they hold among them the millionaire's capital,
and have sufficient intelligence, honesty, thorough reliability,
and consequent thorough reliance upon each other, to combine
it, to carry on the business from which he derives his income,
so that their earnings shall average 140*l.* per year, the amount
of labour which they will demand in their more comfortable
position will not only be greater, but of a nature very much
superior and more stable than that demanded by the master's
luxuriousness. In all cases of commercial panic and depression,
it is those who minister to luxury who are first dispensed with.
The system of co-operation, carried out to the full, would
cause, not the annihilation of the labours of the five and a
half millions of workers, whom we have shown to be working
entirely for the luxuries of wealth, but the transfer of a portion of it to immensely worthier and more useful objects. An
advance in the morality of the working classes, sufficient to
enable them to co-operate in the highest sense of the term,

would mean the thousands of workmen engaged in the production of alcohol and other degrading popular luxuries withdrawn
from their present wasteful occupations and drafted into the
service of a universally elevated style of life—the land tilled
and mined by its owners, o'erlooked, mayhap, by fewer baronial
piles filled with costly luxuries, yet assuredly not hiding in its
out-of-the-way corners and neglected patches the squalid hovels
of a debased peasantry, but covered with smiling homesteads,
in which millions could enjoy all the necessaries and elegances
of a civilised life—it would mean the profits of the factory and
the warehouse shared in by the mechanic and the clerk,
perhaps fewer new palatial squares and crescents, but certainly
the widening out of the narrow lanes and close alleys of our
great cities—it might mean the building of fewer yachts and
the beautifying of more ships, the yacht's crew drafted, a third
watch, into the merchantman, and the conversion of our
mercantile navy from sordid traffickers, with crews wrought
and housed like dogs, into the stately pleasure craft of commerce, sailed and navigated by the owners—it might mean
many of the great lords of the manors' retinue of lacqueys and
the millionaire's swarm of servants changed into profitable
workers, lifting off the overweight of toil from the shoulders
of their fellows, or engaged in the multiplicity of artistic
occupations demanded by the community in their more elevated style of living—in a word, it would mean every wholesome necessary, along with leisure, education, refinement—
*Civilisation of the Masses.*

And this elevation of the standard of living of the working
classes, by means of their own industry, sobriety, and self-
denial, would certainly not imply a curtailment of the manly,
healthy, and useful luxuries of the rich, but would be accompanied by a corresponding advance amongst all classes, and
the beneficial gradation in the modes of living would still be
maintained.

The bulk of the working classes are as yet, however, far
from having attained to anything like the elevation of moral
tone requisite for this system of labour, and are for the present
safer under the tutelage of the capitalist. In the wasteful
hands of the luxurious majority, including a great number of
the rich, incapable of taking care of their wealth, and continually gravitating downwards to become the poorest of the poor,
even the vast capital of this, the wealthiest nation under the
sun, the foundation of our splendid commercial supremacy,

would melt away in the course of a few years with nothing but misery to show for result ; and the rent of the land, which Mr. Henry George seeks to appropriate, would be but as a drop in the bucket : but there is a continually increasing minority, possessing all the moral qualifications, and who are training themselves step by step in the necessary business experience for its development ; and if we believe that our civilisation will yet become permeated by the principles of Christianity, and that in the wake of Christianity must follow practical material benefit, we need not despair of such high results ; and the recent advances towards this goal must be hailed with satisfaction, as the first rays of diviner light upon their dim and narrow horizon, the dawn of a glorious day which is yet to shine upon them.

## CHAPTER IV.

### PROGRESS.

(The substance of this chapter was delivered as a Lecture on the inauguration of Renton Mechanics' Institution, 1882.)

BUT, in spite of luxuriousness and other vices, the grand moral influences of Christianity, permeating every fibre of our social life, have been impelling the nation slowly, steadily, and surely forward in the path of progress. The existence of a golden age in the past, from which the present has sadly degenerated, is one of those beautiful poetical myths which the searching investigation of modern days has almost entirely dispelled. Perhaps more of this halo of sentiment and romance has been shed around the condition of the Highlanders of Scotland under their clan system than that of any other people, and yet the 'Crofters' Commissioners,' in their 'Report,' recently published, say :—

'We remain under the impression that, while in the whole community there was a larger proportionate number of persons living in rude comfort in former times, there was also a larger number in a condition of precarious indigence. The average amount of moral and material welfare is as great now as at any previous period, and the poorest class were never so well protected against the extremities of human suffering.'

Except in the case of a few who say that 'the former days were better than these,' but who do 'not inquire wisely concerning this' (Eccles. vii. 10), men who have arrived at middle age cannot fail to notice the improvement which has been going on around them, and which to older men is even much more striking.

Even Ruskin, than whom there is no keener critic of modern society, confesses that the present youthful female beauty of Britain's better classes—no mean index of physical and moral progress—excels all that has gone before it as preserved in portraits by masters' hands.

Than the Earl of Shaftesbury there was no more practical observer of our social conditions, past and present, or one more capable of giving an opinion on the subject, and in his examination by 'The Dwellings Commission,' lately, he stated that he was able to testify to the enormous improvement that has taken place in the poorest districts of London within his memory.[1]

In regard to Glasgow also he expressed his great admiration and satisfaction with what had been done there.

Mr. Giffen, President of the Statistical Society, in his recent pamphlet on 'The Progress of the Working Classes,' says :—

'Dropping statistics for the moment, I should like to give my own testimony to an observed fact of social life—that there is nothing so striking or so satisfactory to those who can carry their memories back forty years as to observe the superiority of the education of the masses at the present time to what it was then.'

In the chapter on 'Leisure' I have alluded at length to the enormous improvement in the hours of labour, especially for women, young persons, and children, which has taken place since 1833 through the beneficial action of our 'factory legislation,' and I now simply mention it as a fundamental and most important part of our progress. In this respect we are far ahead of our Continental neighbours and of the United States.

[1] He told, for example, how he remembered cases in which the husband and wife had to sit up alternately at night to keep the rats, which came into the room from the sewer in swarms of a score at a time, away from the children, and how it was quite a common experience to find cesspools not more than a single foot below rooms teeming with families.

The 'weaker vessels' have been among the first to reap the benefits derived from lessened toil, and the average duration of their lives has been increased three and a half years (as compared with two years for males) within the last forty years. The improved appearance of the children in factories, who, while being carefully guarded from overwork, are being educated in a superior manner,[1] has been a subject of the most satisfactory remark to myself and all who have had any practical experience of our factories.

In the preceding chapters I have alluded to intemperance as the besetting sin and crushing drawback of the British workman and shown how it interferes in every way with his efficiency, remuneration, comfort, and improvement, but bad as things still are in this respect there has been much progress, due in a great measure to the temperance societies.

Fifty years ago, for instance, the money which each apprentice was forced to pay on the completion of his apprenticeship was almost invariably squandered in the most severe bacchanalian orgies, whilst a regular system of smuggling drink into the works during work hours was continually going on.

Now, very much owing to the influence and example of the 'temperance men,' there is very much higher moral tone amongst the great majority of our tradesmen, and in my own experience this has been productive of splendid practical results.

The provost of the neighbouring burgh of Dumbarton, conversing with me as to this elevation of moral tone and improvement of the drinking habits of the working classes, said that in his experience the better class working-man was now as fastidious in shunning the company of the drinking section as men in the higher grades of life used to be not many years ago, amongst whom the reform in their drinking customs has been even more remarkable.

One of the most hopeful signs of our times, the sympathy with which the condition of the more unfortunate of our countrymen is regarded by their richer brethren, will most

---

[1] The chairman of the Glasgow Sabbath School Union, at the annual meeting on April 17, 1884, remarked that the work had not so much drudgery about it as it had twenty-five years ago, when the teachers had a large number of children who had to learn the elements of reading. Now, teachers had higher material at their disposal. While the work in day-schools had been raised, the work in Sabbath-schools had been elevated to the highest Christian teaching.

assuredly evoke reciprocal feelings, and still further cement the union of classes, which has been increasing so much of late. The universal attention given to 'The Bitter Cry of Outcast London,' and the enthusiastic action resulting from it, the formation of 'a committee at Oxford to secure a central residence in London for university men anxious to work among the poor,' the starting of a magazine, 'Eastward Ho!' entirely for the purpose of attracting the interest of the West end of London to the condition of the East end, are all indications of this better feeling.

But, apart from general impressions, the gradual improvement of all classes, and especially of the working classes, during the last fifty years, can be proved by an imposing array of facts and statistics.[1]

Whilst investigating the luxury of 1884 (this being the latest year for which I have been able to collect statistics) as compared with that of 1870 (the year for which the chapter on this subject was contributed to 'Fraser,' and about which time probably the culminating point of Britain's wealthy and popular luxuriousness was reached), though prepared for improvement, I was most agreeably surprised by the extent of the progress which a study of the statistics of many of the different items successively disclosed.

The first to be noted, and one of the most important steps in advance during the fourteen years comprising this period, has been the increase of the average income of the working classes from 33s. to 36s. per week per family, being about 9 per cent. in money value, whilst the purchasing power of money for food, clothing, and houses has increased in an even greater ratio, by the cheapening of all kinds of commodities, in great measure owing to the reduction of the profits of capital, and the level of necessaries has been most materially and beneficially raised, probably to the extent of 20 per cent. to 25 per cent.[2]

The second item of importance to be noted is the extraordinary increase in the number of our middle classes and the consequent beneficial diffusion of wealth over a far larger area.

In 1870 there were not more than 450,000 persons (who, with their families, numbered about 2,000,000) with in-

---

[1] See Note 1 in Appendix to 'Progress.'

[2] In this country it cost a labourer, to procure enough to pay for a bushel of wheat, 5 days' labour in 1770; 4 in 1843; 2½ in 1870; 2 now.

comes of 200*l*. per annum and upwards, whilst in 1884 there were about 750,000, who, with their families, numbered about 3½ millions, being an increase of 75 per cent., whilst the population increased only about 20 per cent.

This statement seemed to me at first almost too good to be true, but I have verified it not only by the income-tax returns, but by a comparison of the number of dwelling-houses with a rental of 20*l*. and upwards at these different periods. In 1870 they were 450,679 ; in 1884, 809,271. I find also that the 'Final Report of the Royal Commission appointed to inquire into the Depression of Trade and Industry,' and just issued as I was revising this chapter, affords strong corroboration, and some of their more important remarks I have embodied in the Appendix.[1]

What an incalculable amount of loyal contentment, steady prosperity, and solid comfort and happiness has not only been effected, but is yet in store for the nation by this beneficent diffusion of wealth, this grand spread of the means of education, culture, and refinement !

The next item of importance in progress to be educed from this comparison of statistics is that, with a population which has increased about 20 per cent., and with an income which has increased about 40 per cent., the expenditure upon intoxicating liquors has decreased by almost 7½ per cent., and that whilst the average earnings of the working classes per family have advanced from 85*l*. to 93*l*. per annum, their expenditure upon intoxicating liquors has decreased by about 2*l*. per family.

This is one of the many satisfactory indications of progress to which the Commissioners on the Depression of Trade refer in the following words : ' There is no feature in the situation which we have been called upon to examine so satisfactory as the immense improvement which has taken place in the condition of the working classes during the last twenty years. At the present moment there is, as we have already pointed out, a good deal of distress owing to the want of regular work, but there can be no question that the workman in this country is, when fully employed, in almost every respect in a better position than his competitors in foreign countries, and we think that no diminution in our productive capacity has resulted from this improvement in his position.'

In the ' Contemporary Review ' for February 1882 there is a

---

[1] See Note 2 in Appendix to ' Progress.'

remarkable statistical article, entitled, 'The Rise of the Middle Class,' by Mr. M. G. Mulhall. Though condensed into a few pages, it contains the most interesting and conclusive statistical account of our economic progress which I have seen, and must have taken the writer months of research. The principal object of the article is to show that, instead of 'the rich growing richer and the poor poorer,' as asserted by some 'social reformers,' who 'do not think it necessary to bring forward a single proof in support of their fallacy,' 'the rich are not individually so wealthy as before, while the proportion of persons in middle fortune has doubled, and the condition of the working classes improved in even greater degree than the growth of capital.'[1]

In a series of most interesting statistical tables he shows that this more equable diffusion of wealth has been going on throughout the whole of Europe, and pre-eminently in our own country. While the rich and the middle classes in the United Kingdom are far more numerous and influential, the condition of the working classes also is very much superior, they being much better fed and otherwise more prosperous than in any other country.

The following table shows the ratio of each class, and average income in the various countries :—

|  | Ratio | | | Average | | |
|---|---|---|---|---|---|---|
|  | Rich | Middle | Working | Rich | Middle | Working |
|  |  |  |  | £ | £ | £ |
| United Kingdom . | 3·36 | 27·33 | 69·31 | 1500 | 260 | 100 |
| France . . . . . | 2·05 | 21·64 | 76·31 | 800 | 200 | 85 |
| Germany . . . . | 1·28 | 7·30 | 91·42 | 734 | 160 | 76 |
| Italy . . . . . | 0·55 | 3·57 | 95·88 | 520 | 60 | 40 |
| Spain . . . . . | 0·72 | 3·88 | 95·40 | 880 | 140 | 43 |
| Russia[2] . . . . . | 0·15 | 0·75 | 99·10 | 3800 | 200 | 33 |

In addition to the above 'sectional view of society, showing the thickness of the three strata,' Mr. Mulhall gives the following, 'showing the ratio of collective income in the various countries falling to each class,' and deduces as 'worthy of

---

[1] Mr. Hoyle remarks that, according to Mr. Mann, a spinner in 1760 could only earn from 2s. to 3s. weekly; whereas now he can earn from 30s. to 35s. weekly.

[2] Where there are only princes and peasants.

special notice that in countries where the earnings of the
working class form the bulk of national income, as in Russia
and Italy, the people are not so well fed or prosperous as in
those where the working class figures for less, such as Great
Britain and France ; that a nation composed chiefly of hewers
of wood and drawers of water is not to be desired, and that
the more we endeavour to make machinery supply the place
of manual labour the more we exalt the mass and improve the
condition of society.'

|  | Millions Sterling | | | Ratio | | |
|---|---|---|---|---|---|---|
|  | Rich | Middle | Working | Rich | Middle | Working |
| United Kingdom . | 334 | 468 | 463 | 26·40 | 37·10 | 36·50 |
| France . . . . . | 127 | 333 | 505 | 13·20 | 34·40 | 52·40 |
| Germany . . . . | 88 | 110 | 652 | 10·35 | 12·95 | 76·70 |
| Italy . . . . . . | 16 | 12 | 214 | 6·66 | 5·00 | 88·34 |
| Spain . . . . . | 22 | 19 | 144 | 11·90 | 10·30 | 77·80 |
| Russia . . . . . | 92 | 25 | 526 | 14·40 | 3·90 | 81·70 |
| Total . . . . | 679 | 967 | 2,504 | 16·40 | 23·35 | 60·25 |

These tables, compiled by Mr. Mulhall, are worthy of the
most careful attention, as showing our economical position as
compared with that of other countries ; and I would draw
special attention to the column in the first table, showing the
average income of the working-men of the various European
nationalities, which shows that the wages of French working-
men are 15 per cent. lower than that of the British ; of
German, 24 per cent. ; of Italian, 60 per cent. ; of Spanish,
57 per cent. ; and of Russian, 67 per cent. ; and this superiority is all the more remarkable, seeing that it is combined
with so much greater leisure, as shown in the chapter on that
subject.

The increase of wealth in the United Kingdom during the
last forty years has been something prodigious, having risen from
3,824 millions in 1840 to 8,420 millions in 1880 ; but, during
that time, instead of the rich growing richer and the poor
poorer, to quote again from Mr. Mulhall's article, ' the average
fortunes of the rich are 11 per cent. lower, those of the middle
class 30 per cent. lower, the result of the spreading of wealth
over a large commercial area, while the condition of the working classes has improved 100 per cent. It is astonishing that,

while the population of the island of Great Britain has risen
63 per cent. since 1840, the wages of workmen, and even of
maidservants, are now 50 per cent. higher. The consumption
of food per inhabitant is the best test of improvement in the
working classes, viz. :—

|  | 1840 | 1880 |
|---|---|---|
| Tea, ozs. . . . . | 22 | 73 |
| Sugar, lbs.. . . . | 15 | 54 |
| Wheat . . . . | 269 | 358 |
| Meat . . . . . | 84 | 118 |

At the same time the increase of depositors in savings-banks
has been from 3 per cent. of population to 10 per cent. ; and
the ratio of paupers has fallen to 3 per cent. of the inhabitants of the United Kingdom, the lowest known since the
beginning of the century.'

In Great Britain the value of house property has grown
much faster than population, the average per house having
risen 75 per cent. since 1851. (Mulhall's 'History of Prices,'
p. 109.)

' As a further instance of improvement, the persons unable
to sign the marriage register fell from 42 per cent. in 1840, to
23 per cent. in 1878.'

' The "levelling up" of the middle and lower orders has
been as gradual and steady as the growth of national wealth.'

This he proves from a variety of Government returns.

In a pamphlet on 'The Progress of the Working Classes in
the Last Half-Century,' by Mr. Robert Giffen, President of
the Statistical Society,[1] he considers that 'the workman gets
from 50 to 100 per cent. more money for 20 per cent. less
work ; in round figures, he has gained from 70 to 120 per cent.
in fifty years in money return,' and that in this proportion he
is better fed, better clothed, and better housed ; that he pays
less taxes and gets more—much more—from the Government.
He shows, also, from an able paper on 'The Recent Decline
in the English Death-rate,'[2] by Mr. Humphreys, that 'the
effect of the decline' (which he proves) 'is to raise the mean
duration of life among males from 39·9 to 41·9 years, a gain
of two years in the average duration of life, and among females
from 41·9 to 45·3 years, a gain of nearly three years in the
average duration of life.' ' Mr. Humphreys also showed that by
far the larger proportion of the increased duration of human life

[1] London: George Bell and Sons, York Street, Covent Garden.
[2] *Statistical Society's Journal*, vol. xlvi. p. 195.

PROGRESS 81

in England is lived at useful ages, and not at the dependent ages of either childhood or old age. This little statement is absolutely conclusive on the subject ; but we are apt to over-look how much the figures mean. No such change could take place without a great increase in the vitality of the people. Not only have fewer died, but the masses who have lived must have been healthier, and have suffered less from sickness than they did.' 'From the nature of the figures the improvement must have been among the masses and not among a select class, whose figures throw up the average. The figures to be affected relate to such large masses of population that so great a change in the average could not have occurred if only a small percent-age of the population had improved in health.'

Mr. Giffen also points out 'that the improvement in health actually recorded obviously relates to a transition stage. Many of the improvements in the condition of the working classes have taken place only quite recently. They have not, therefore, affected all through their existence any but the youngest lives. When the improvements have been in exist-ence for a longer period, so that the lives of all who are living must have been affected from birth by the changed conditions, we may infer that even a greater gain in the mean duration of life will be shown. As it is the gain is enormous.'

And Mr. Mulhall states that the better health 'of our people enables us to work at greater advantage than most other nations.'

As to education, 'the children of the masses in England are, in fact, now obtaining a good education all round ; while, fifty years ago, they had either no education at all or a com-paratively poor one ;' whilst 'in Scotland the superiority of the common school system is immensely superior to what it was forty years since.'

The latest improvement in education has been the intro-duction, by order of the Education Department, of drawing as a class subject.

This early introduction to art in our elementary schools should have a great effect on British workmanship, both in our own home surroundings and in that keen competition with foreign countries of which I am going to speak further on, and the workmen of the future will have a great advantage over those of the present and the past.

'As to crime, the facts to note are that, rather more than

G

forty years ago, with a population little more than half what
it is now, the number of criminal offenders committed for trial
(1839) was 54,000; in England alone, 24,000. Now the
corresponding figures are—United Kingdom, 22,000; and
England, 15,000; fewer criminals by a great deal in a much
larger population.'

'As regards pauperism, since 1849 we have continuous
figures, and from these we know that, with a constantly increasing population, there is an absolute decline in the amount
of pauperism. The earliest and latest figures are :—Of paupers
in receipt of relief in the United Kingdom in 1849, 1,676,000;
in 1881, 1,014,000.[1]

In savings-banks there has been 'an increase of tenfold'
in the number of depositors, and of fivefold and more in the
amount of deposits.

Regarding the enormous increase of co-operative societies,
I am speaking at length in the next chapter.[2]

Pre-eminent in this race of improvement, and far outstrip-
ping any of her competitors, is our own country of Scotland.
To quote again from Mr. Mulhall :—'It is remarkable that
Scotland possesses more wealth for population, and has become
the richest country in the world, though so poorly gifted by
Nature. Her fortune has quintupled since 1840, being now
double that of Ireland. We may search European annals since
the time of Alexander of Macedon, and we shall find nothing
to equal the rise of Scotland in the above period. But it is a
fact of which Scotland seems unaware ; at least, they never
mention it. The increase of wealth per inhabitant is much
less striking in England than in the sister kingdom, the condition of the latter having undergone a wonderful change.
Forty years ago Scotland swarmed with beggars to such an
extent that the sheriffs declared that the state of the country

---

[1] See Note 3 in Appendix to 'Progress.'

[2] In quoting at length from two such eminent statistical authorities
as Mr. Mulhall and Mr. Giffen, it is worthy of note that, in estimating
the ratio of economic progress, the former estimates the sovereign as
'having lost half-a-crown in purchasing power since 1840,' which he
verifies by an interesting table showing that the yearly consumption for
a family of five persons (according to the present average, though much
lower then) in 1840 would cost 92l. 14s., in 1880 106l. 4s., whilst the
latter's 'conclusion is that, taking things in the mass, the sovereign
goes as far as it did forty or fifty years ago, while there are many new
things in existence at a low price which could not then have been
bought at all.'

was most alarming, and the farmers were so poor that they bled their cattle and cooked the blood for food !'

People are living yet amongst us who remember that bodies of men used to go round in the spring to lift the emaciated cattle on to their feet, and assist them to the pasture. 'Now all that is changed, and such is the prosperity of the bulk of the people that Scotland has now an average of 277*l.* per head of population, as against England's 262*l.*, being 15*l.* per head greater.' 'Puir auld Scotland' is no longer the correct designation of our fatherland, and if we take into account the enormous number of wealthy Scotchmen in England, in the Colonies, and scattered throughout the world, our commercial position is not unlike that of the Jews ; but 'the Scot abroad' well sustains the reputation of his country for honesty, straightforward dealing, and other good qualities, which render him everywhere popular in spite of the sneers at his so-called money-grubbing propensities. So notorious is the fact in England, that a Scotchman stepping on the lowest rung of the ladder is sure to climb to the highest, that a facetious Lancashire manufacturer, on being applied to for a humble clerkship in his large office by a poor Scotch lad, told him that he did not want a partner.

Now, I wish to point out to you some of the principal causes which have led to these very extraordinary and happy results. There are many economists who would simply tell you that it is all owing to the introduction of steam-power, and the great mineral wealth of Scotland, which has enabled her to turn it to good account ; but this is a very near-sighted and materialistic view of the subject. Other countries are far more richly endowed with the elements of material prosperity, even with minerals, than Scotland.

It is to the superior physical power,[1] to the industry, to

---

[1] From Mulhall's *Dictionary of Statistics :*—

HEIGHT OF BRITISH ARMY (1882).

| — | English | Scotch | Irish |
|---|---|---|---|
| Over 6 ft. . . . . . . . | 0·6 | 1·2 | 0·3 |
| 5 ft. 10 in. to 6 ft. . . . . . | 11·0 | 11·2 | 8·3 |
| 5 ft. 6 in. to 5 ft. 10 in. . . . . | 41·1 | 42·6 | 36·1 |
| Under 5 ft. 6 in. . . . . . . | 47·3 | 45·0 | 55·3 |

the intelligence,[1] and, above all, to the morality of her people, that Scotland stands in her present proud position.[2]

It has been recently proved that oatmeal,[3] of all regular diets, is the best fitted for giving a sturdy muscularity and large bonedness, which are characteristic of the Scottish workman, and render him unequalled where hard work is concerned ; and I have referred in the chapter on 'Luxury' to the deleterious effects resulting from abandoning simple and nutritious articles of food for more luxurious diet.

Of the causes which have conduced to give Scotchmen the intelligence which has been one of the main causes of their success, first and foremost, there was the splendid system of the parochial schools, putting within reach of the poorest inhabitant the means of educating his family, and of which there were very few who did not take advantage. This system was, however, suited only for a rural and comparatively stationary population ; but with the enormous increase of our manufacturing industries it seemed likely to be altogether swamped by the great influx of an Irish labouring population. The provisions of the new Education Act are, however, enabling us to grapple most successfully, I think, with this difficulty, and the education of the rising generation of all classes is undoubtedly far superior to that of their fathers, whilst in England whole classes are being well taught who were before left in entire ignorance.

Conspicuous amongst the other educational agencies of the present century are Mechanics' Institutions. When begun,

---

[1]. The latest classification of races, according to Bastian and other experts, shows weight of brain as follows :—

| | Ounces | | | Ounces |
|---|---|---|---|---|
| Scotch | 50 | Pawnees | | 47·1 |
| Germans | 49·6 | Italians | | 46·9 |
| English | 49·5 | Hindu | | 45·1 |
| French | 47·9 | Gypsy | | 44·8 |
| Zulus | 47·5 | Bushmen | | 44·6 |
| Chinese | 47·2 | Esquimaux | | 43·9 |

[2] See Note 4 in Appendix to 'Progress.'

[3] Frankland's table of food required to lift a man (ten stone) 10,000 feet :—

| | Pounds | Cost |
|---|---|---|
| Beef | 3·58 | 36 pence |
| Bread | 2·35 | 5 „ |
| Flour | 1·31 | 4 „ |
| Oatmeal | 1·28 | 3 „ |

they were intended to be schools of severe study for the working classes, and to deal almost entirely with scientific subjects; but there has been a wide departure from the original intention,[1] and they are now, at least as far as their public lectures are concerned, made the means principally for literary and musical recreation, no mean end to subserve for men and women who have been employed for ten hours in some mechanical occupation. The adjuncts necessary for a proper Mechanics' Institute are, first, a good hall, secondly, a good library, and, thirdly, a good course of lectures. Books by themselves are good, and a vast amount of information may be derived from their perusal, but their value is very much enhanced when the thoughtful reader is brought into personal contact with superior and more highly-trained minds; and almost every village community in the country is provided with these means of intellectual progress by its Mechanics' Institute.

Supplementary to the public course of lectures, there.. are now in connection with many Mechanics' Institutes a number of science classes, which educate in special scientific and practical subjects in an even more thorough manner than in the olden time.

The spread of art amongst all classes of the country, with its educating and refining influences, is a subject of general remark. But in music especially, which touches more deeply and tenderly, and altogether universally, the popular heart, this progress has been most remarkable. Music is now one of the regular branches of education and recreation, and a most valuable one in all schools, from the infant department to the highest standard. Sabbath-schools are trained to sing correctly and scientifically in unison, and to vie with each other in the artistic rendering of beautiful hymn-tunes. The singing in unison by the children of the noble psalms and hymns in which they are instructed must exercise an incalculable amount of the highest moral influence upon them, continue with them all their lives, and be transmitted through the centuries until it merges in the transcendent hallelujah chorus of eternity. Associations for the cultivation of music are in connection

---

[1] I have been favoured with the first bill of the Vale of Leven Mechanics' Institution for the session 1838-9, which is very interesting, and the course of lectures bears out what I have said, and is in marked contrast for solidity to the present one and to our Renton one.

with almost every church, and elsewhere they are abounding more and more.

To the Church itself, which has preached a stern morality to the people, encouraged them in the way of uprightness, and keenly exercised their intellects on the loftiest of all topics, Scotland has been more indebted than to any other cause in bringing about her material prosperity, by causing the people to ' seek first the Kingdom of God and His righteousness,' so that all these things were added to them.

That there is unhappily still a great deal of vice, and especially of intemperance, amongst us no one can deny ; but it is equally certain that the moral agencies at work are more than coping with them. ' The convictions in the years 1840–42 averaged 1,120 per million inhabitants yearly, and in 1876–80 only 570 per million, a decline of nearly 50 per cent., owing to which sixteen Scotch prisons have been recently closed for want of occupants.'—(Mulhall's ' Rise and Progress of the Middle Class.')

Nothing could more satisfactorily attest our progress in ' the righteousness which exalteth a nation,' and of which so many corroborative facts have already been furnished.

The progress of Scotland in material and moral well-being has been specially alluded to as being the most remarkable, but, though excelling, she has been by no means solitary. Like a mighty army, and at the word of command from the Lord of Hosts, all the great nationalities have made a simultaneous advance into a higher life. Their progress has, indeed, been slow—infinitely slow—except to the eye of Him to whom ' a thousand years are but as one day, and one day as a thousand years,' but sure and steadfast ; nor will it cease until the glorious ' latter days ' arise upon the earth.

Well may the subjects of Queen Victoria celebrate with grateful happy hearts the auspicious year of her jubilee and the unexampled progress which has marked the fifty years of her benignant reign.

With deep gratitude for the past and unfaltering faith for the future, let us view our present position, and calmly, resolutely, and intelligently seek out and practise the best means for further progress.

The steps in *economic progress* which, in my opinion, should be taken first, will be treated of in the next chapter, ' On the Acquisition of Property by the Working Classes.'

# CHAPTER V.

## ON THE ACQUISITION OF PROPERTY BY THE WORKING CLASSES.

(A Lecture delivered to the Renton Mechanics' Institution, 1884, being in the opinion of the lecturer the very best advice on the subject he could give to the workpeople in the employment of his firm, and, with such minor modifications as different localities may require, to the manufacturing population throughout the country, and was, he believes, endorsed by the opinions of the intelligent working-men of the district.

For a number of the figures quoted I am indebted to Mulhall's 'Dictionary of Statistics,' [1] an admirable compendium of statistical information.)

THE title of this lecture, 'The Acquisition of Property by the Working Classes,' shows that it belongs to the dry region of political economy, and it is doubtless far less attractive than many others in this course. 'Property!' I think I hear some of the more poetical souls of Renton exclaim, 'a sorry subject with which to entertain a body of working-men after their day's toil,' and resort naturally to the stirring lines of our national poet, Burns :—

> Is there, for honest poverty,
>     That hangs his head, and a' that !
> The coward slave, we pass him by,
>     We dare be poor for a' that !
> For a' that, and a' that,
>     Our toils obscure, and a' that ;
> The rank is but the guinea's stamp,
>     The man's the gowd for a' that !
>
> What tho' on hamely fare we dine,
>     Wear hoddin gray, and a' that ;
> G'ie fools their silks, and knaves their wine,
>     A man's a man for a' that !
> For a' that, and a' that,
>     Their tinsel show, and a' that ;
> The honest man, though e'er sae poor,
>     Is king o' men for a' that !

Now, I will at the very outset disarm my sentimental critics by admitting frankly that these manly words express my own ideas in far superior language, and that my subject is not one of the first rank, neither of the second, but quite of the third,

---

[1] London : George Routledge & Sons.

inasmuch as that portion of the material world which we can portion out into shares is subsidiary to the body to which it ministers, whilst the body is the humble adjunct of the immortal part ; and in these relative positions they must ever stand, attended by their professions of law, medicine, and divinity—law for property, medicine for health, divinity for morals.  But when I show you, as I think I can, that very much of health, yes, and very much of morality, are bound up in this question of property, I hope you may be able to derive from my remarks, if not amusement, at least some practical instruction.  The division of property—the apportioning of it amongst the various tribes and nations who people the world, and its more minute subdivision amongst the various classes and individuals who compose these peoples—has been the cause of more strife and contention than anything else in the world's history.  In earlier and more lawless times property was divided by—

> The good old rule, the simple plan,
>   That they should take who have the power,
>   And they should keep who can.

'This is mine ; ' 'Nay, but it is mine,' are the natural and universal 'watchword and reply,' prompted by the strong egoism implanted in every human breast where a question of ownership is concerned.  In the very dawn of history, when the world had not an inhabitant to each 1,000 square miles, the covetous eye of the painted hunter rested upon some patch of territory more advantageous than his own, and the owner had to quit or defend it at the cost of blood.  As individuals coalesced and grew into tribes and nations, the same tragedies were enacted again and again on a larger scale.  It is not so very long since—in fact, in the time of the grandfathers of some of those present—when Rob Roy and his band of armed caterans used to swoop down into this very vale, and retreat with stores of plundered cattle and forage to his Highland fastnesses ; and over a great portion of the globe this style of things is still the order of the day.  Even in Europe, the most civilised part of the world, over three millions of men, armed to the teeth, stand around the frontiers of her States to defend their property, and over two hundred thousand in armour-plated ships of war sweep round its coasts for the same purpose.

Any progress in civilisation has been the accompaniment,

and in large measure the result, of greater respect for property
and better protection of it. Whenever individuals or communities are uncertain that they may reap the fruits of their
labours their industry slackens off, and they will almost rather
starve than produce what has a chance to be consumed by
lawless rapacity. Recognising this fact, property in all
countries which have made any progress in civilisation is
hedged about with stern and inexorable law, which, however
hard it may bear on individual cases, is absolutely necessary
for the existence of society. But though property in our own
and other civilised countries is not now divided in the same
rough and bloody fashion, yet contest for its possession is continually going on in many ways—the buyer strives to get as
much for his money as he can, the seller to give as little;
workmen strive to obtain the highest wages from their employers, who, in their turn, pressed by their competitors in the
markets of the world, seek to get labour at its lowest price;
and this, as you are aware, is called the struggle between
labour and capital, which sometimes culminates in those
bitter strifes called strikes, a subject to which I will refer
further on.

The French Communists would tell you that 'property is
theft,' and that everything of value should belong to the
community, and not to the individual. In a recent number
of the French anarchist journal, 'Drapeau Noir,' a violent
article, after enjoining the use of the dagger, poison, and
dynamite for the destruction of capitalists, adds :—'We shall
soon be able to appease our thirst for vengeance, and to destroy at our ease all these parasites. Let us then be stirring,
for time presses. Let us massacre our employers. Let us
burn their properties. The most terrible means are the best,
and let our motto always be, "Ni Dieu, ni maître."' The
shrewd common sense which is so characteristic of Scotchmen
has always, however, enabled the vast majority of Scottish
working-men to perceive that whenever you make property
common, it is to have it squandered by the vicious, the foolish,
and the intemperate, at the expense of the frugal, the honest,
and the industrious; and it is on account of their better
education and superior intelligence that it is possible for an
employer to meet with them and discuss, I hope without
friction, a question so closely allied with the interests of both
—a discussion which might be attended with unpleasantness
in almost any other country at the present time.

When this institution was inaugurated, about a year ago, I endeavoured to show you the solid progress which has been going on in the wages and general living of the working classes of this country during the last forty years, and I will not further refer to this, my object in this lecture being to try to show you how to improve in a much greater degree your material prosperity. To begin our investigations we will take a look at the various kinds of property in the country, and the value of each. The property of the United Kingdom amounts in round numbers to 8,720 millions sterling, divided as follows :—Land, 1,880 millions ; houses, 2,280 millions, constituting considerably the largest item ; railways, 770 millions ; shipping, 120 millions ; merchandise, 350 millions ; furniture, 1,140 millions ; bullion, 143 millions ; loans, 1,060 millions ; sundries, 563 millions—total, 8,720 millions, only a very small proportion of which is owned by the working classes, who constitute nearly two-thirds of the population. It is difficult to determine how much is owned by them exactly. The funds of friendly and building societies, about 56 millions ; of co-operative societies, about 7 millions ; and deposits in savings-banks, about 80 millions ; in all 143 millions must belong almost entirely to them ; and if we estimate their other and more private property, of which there is no record, at double this amount, their total property would be about 430 millions—only one-twentieth of the whole. But this can only be a rough estimate. Now, it is going to be my aim in this lecture to show working people how to acquire a much larger proportion of this property, and to which of these classes of property they should first direct their attention, and—

1. *They have to provide themselves with food, wholesome in quality, plentiful in quantity, and temperately partaken of ;*

2. *With clothing, healthy, comfortable, and durable ;*

3. *With furniture, useful and substantial, and, with respect both to it and clothing, as ornamental as possible ;*

4. *The houses in which they dwell ; and—*

5. *The tools, machinery, workshops, factories, lands, ships, &c., requisite for carrying on their daily avocations.*

The first and second classes of property—viz. food and clothing—the working classes already possess in one form or another, and I do not intend to allude to them further than to say that the change in the diet of working people, from simple and nutritious meals to stimulating and innutritious tea and coffee beverages, partaken of three or four times a day, is not a beneficial one, and that milk and soup should again be reinstated in their old position in the dietary arrangements of you all, especially of the young; and that your clothing should partake less of the flimsy and meretriciously ornamental, prepared principally with a view to outside appearance, and more of the solid, durable, and comfortable, which, while approving of neatness, and ornament, recognises cleanliness, health, and comfort as the prime requisites in all clothing. A judicious and wise economy in regard to the purchase of these two requisites forms a very good basis to start from in striving to acquire property in the other three classes. A respectable Sunday suit for himself and each of his family, in which they could all worship in the sanctuary in decency and order, has long been a distinguishing characteristic of the Scottish working-man, often acquired by him at the cost of considerable privation in his food supplies and other things ; and long may this continue so, and be more imitated by other nationalities. With reference to furniture, it has always been an object of ambition with well-behaved workmen to begin their married life with a fair amount of goodly furniture, and it is only the idle and dissolute—and, let us also bear in mind, the unfortunate—amongst the working classes who do not possess this requisite. Before leaving this subject, let me say that an expenditure upon a well selected though small library, and some objects of art, many of which can now be bought very cheaply, will be wise economy on the part of even the humblest workman. To beautify his home, and make it as attractive to himself and family as his means will afford, should be one of his cherished aims. The associations connected with the home, especially for the children, are permanent, and of far deeper power for good or evil than many people give them credit for.

These three requisites having been provided for, as in the majority of cases they have been, the next property to which the workman should direct his attention is the house he lives in, and after that the capital wherewith to carry on his work. The former of these, viz. his dwelling-house, I will revert to, and most particularly, by-and-by, because it is this class of property the acquisition of which by the working classes I consider to be entirely within the range of present practical political economy, and to the consideration of which I intend most earnestly to call your attention ; but, in the meantime, let us look at the question of the working-man becoming his own capitalist.

The subject of labour and capital is one upon which more has been written during the last forty years than any other, and I have no doubt many of you have perused some of the works on political economy which treat of it. In many of these the antagonism between labour and capital is very strongly dwelt upon ; but in themselves they are mutually necessary and beneficial to each other. One of the simplest forms of capital is a tradesman's tools. Nothing is more necessary and beneficial to the labour of the tradesman—say a joiner or a mason—than a good chest of tools. The tradesman himself is generally the owner of them, and so long as this is the case the labour and the capital are at one ; but should he by any means let them out of his possession, as will sometimes happen, and require to hire them, then separate interests are set up, and the labourer and the capitalist may not agree as to their respective shares of the work produced by these tools without some conflict on the matter. In the same way precisely the complicated machinery of the factory, which now so frequently does the work formerly turned out by the simple tools of the handicraftsman, is capital, and is in itself as necessary and beneficial to the workmen who use it as axe or hammer ; but machinery is far more in the hands of another class. In the beginning of the present century it was very much easier for the individual workman to be his own capitalist than it is at present. The system of work has been gradually changing from the individual working in his own workshop to the factory with its hundreds, and often thousands, of workmen, all combined in one industry, with enormously beneficial economical results. Individual, isolated industrial action is becoming more and more impossible. The time has not so very long gone past when the weaver wrought at his own loom, the smith at his own forge, the carpenter at his own bench. A very few of this class still survive, marking, like fossils, the existence of a bygone period ; but the great work of the country is carried on in far different fashion, and single workmen have no chance in competing with the united labour of the manufactory. Their only chance as capitalists lies in combination—such combination as is practised by the co-operative system. In this system the capital required for carrying on an industry is owned by the workmen, who, after their fixed wages, share the profit or the loss of the business amongst them. The first society was started at Rochdale, in Lancashire, in 1844, with a capital of 28l., and co-operation has progressed very considerably since its introduction. In 1861 there were 66 societies and 38,000 members, with a capital of 365,000*l.*, and sales equal to 1,100,000*l.* ; in 1871, 749 societies, 249,000 members, 2,530,000*l.* of capital, and sales equal to 8,200,000*l.* ; in 1881, 1,118 societies, 1,083,000 members, 6,850,000*l.* capital, and sales equal to 24,400,000*l.* An enormous and most encouraging advance during twenty years, nearly one-fourth of the working classes being now co-operators. The great bulk of these societies, however, exist not for producing merchandise but for selling it, like the co-operative society with which you are acquainted in this district ; and this form of co-operation has been eminently successful. The want of success in productive co-operation is very easily accounted for. To conduct a manufacturing business properly requires a larger amount of intelligence than the mass of the working people possess. But their great want—a want shared by other classes as well—is in the morality necessary for the accumulation and guidance of sufficient capital, and, above all, to enable them to combine and act harmoniously together. Now we will just take as an example our own works. In these works there are over 2,000 people employed, from tradesmen earning a high wage to labourers earning a much lower one, and boys and girls with lower wages still. To accumulate the large capital necessary for carrying on these works by the workers would require an amount of temperance, thrift, self-denial, and wise economy, which you all know as well as I do is beyond the great majority of them, and to combine that capital, and work harmoniously together as co-operators, is still further outside of their present scope of intelligence and morality. Even suppose they were gifted with the money, and asked to carry on the works on their own account, you know very well that such an amount would be so soon withdrawn from capital as to cripple the business at the very start, not to speak of the dissension, bickering, and strife which would inevitably spring up amongst the different partners. One of yourselves—an intelligent tradesman much above the average workers—told me his experience as one of a number of co-operators like himself in the calico-printing business, and the want of union and, consequently, of united action amongst the partners he considered to be one of the great causes of its want of success. There are, I am happy to say, principally in Lancashire, and more particularly in Rochdale, a few co-operative societies which, out of a vast number of failures, survive and flourish, and serve as a bright example to all the working-men of the country of what can be done ; and no one would be better pleased than I myself to see this form of industry increasing. In it is found one of the best. solutions of the differences between labour and capital, and under it strikes become an impossibility. I believe that in the future it will form a much larger factor in the industry of the nation, insuring to its supporters a much more liberal share in the profits of their work. But you must always bear in mind that it requires a very superior class of men for this form of industry, and that the great bulk of the working classes will require long years of education to bring them up to their level. The 'pioneers' of co-operation were men of great intelligence, singular self-denial, and broad views, and the men who wish to follow in their steps must see that they are like-minded. I am glad to think that many of the working-men of Renton are quite up to this standard, but in an industry like ours there are far more much below it. Many of the more advanced school of political economists, forgetting that a nation cannot be educated to a new form of industry in the course of a year or two, but takes generations to effect any radical change, thought that the new order of things would be at once generally adopted, and many generous employers, impregnated with this idea, were found willing to accelerate it by adopting the system in their works ; but in almost every case they were bitterly disappointed with the result, their men having neither sufficient intelligence nor morality for this superior form of working.

Distributive co-operation—that is, the co-operation which exists for the sale of products—is the very best training which the working people can have for the more difficult and, to them, much more advantageous form of it, viz., productive co-operation ; and it is a very pleasing sign of the times that such a large proportion of them have embarked in this most educative enterprise, and that their number and capital is so very strongly on the increase. In it they are being practically trained in all the principles and details of sound mercantile business—in economy and self-denial, to enable them to save the necessary capital and to pay ready money for what they purchase—in self-reliance and in respect and trust of their fellow co-operators, to combine their savings—in rectitude of dealing amongst themselves and with those who sell to them, and in the intelligence which enables them to conduct their business with success alongside of individual competition, and

I cordially recommend it to all working-men. Another most admirable form of economy, which is being more and more largely practised by the working classes, is the investment of their means in friendly societies. These are formed on the principle that a man in his prime should make provision for the wants of old age, and that in health something be laid by for the time of sickness. At present there are of friendly societies in Great Britain, 15,379, with 4,692,000 members, and funds amounting to 12,750,000*l.*; of provident societies there are 1,587, with 716,000 members, and a capital of 6,337,000*l.*; of building societies, 1,268, with 372,000 members, and a capital of 37,080,000*l.* Including non-registered societies the estimated number of members is seven millions, or one-fifth of the population; 56 per cent. men, and 44 per cent. women. In ten years the Oddfellows and Foresters have increased 310,000, and the funds over two millions sterling. I need not say how much I approve of such societies, as our firm has given practical evidence of its feeling in the matter by subscribing for a long number of years to a friendly society in connection with the works. But while advocating the claims of each and all of these means for acquiring property, *I wish most emphatically and particularly to direct your attention to the acquisition as your own property of your own dwelling-houses.* The proper housing of the working classes has become recently the most prominent question of the day. It is exercising the attention of philanthropists in all classes, and our leading politicians on both sides are eagerly discussing it. I have no doubt many of you have read 'The Bitter Cry of Outcast London,' a production which has caused a sensation throughout the kingdom, unequalled since Tom Hood wrote his 'Song of the Shirt,' and which has opened the eyes of many of the upper classes to a fearful and horrible state of matters, long familiar to all who have taken any interest in social reform. I have no doubt also but that many of you have seen digests in the daily papers of two articles on 'Labourers' and Artisans' Dwellings,' the one in the 'National Review' for November, by Lord Salisbury, and the other in the 'Fortnightly Review' for December, by Mr. Chamberlain. Each of these deals with extraneous aid which may be afforded to the working classes for their proper housing. The schemes therein propounded it is not within the limits of this lecture to discuss, and I will not further refer to them than by saying that we should welcome all efficient aid in the solving of this vast problem from whatever source it may come, whether from the State, from the landowner, or from the employer of labour ; but I wish most earnestly to impress upon all working-men that, no matter what assistance they may get from the outside, the principal, most satisfactory, and only permanent solution of the question lies almost entirely with themselves.   The State may interfere for the protection of the working classes in the amount of space and other sanitary conditions in the erection of their dwellings, and wise legislation can do much, but if the dwellers be vicious or intemperate, no laws on earth can save them from the physical degradation which must surround them ; landowners may erect hundreds of cottages on the most approved principles, but if the peasant occupiers besot themselves in the village alehouse, these cottages will form for a short time but a fair outside show—squalor and filth will soon reign within and around ; and manufacturers may build row upon row of such dwellings as are considered most suitable for their workpeople, but unless they have been educated to some sense of decency, to temperance and domestic virtue, it is but money thrown away.   The better housing of the working classes, like all other economic problems, must be viewed chiefly from a moral standpoint.   I wish to put before you the immensely superior advantages, over all other schemes, of labourers and artisans possessing their own houses, the source from which the funds to buy or build them is to be derived, and the best method of applying these funds.   Regarding the advantages of a working-man owning his own house.   In the first place, the occupier knows much better than anyone else what is suitable for himself and family.   Landlords sometimes, even with the best intentions, erect very strange houses for tenants.   The workman in erecting his own house will be able to study to the minutest detail everything that adds to his own convenience and comfort.   In the second place, as owners they will take much better care of their dwellings than as occupiers merely.   Landlords know by bitter experience that every degree of damage to their property is perpetrated by thoughtless and malicious tenants, even to the burning of doors and shutters by the thriftless class, who do not hesitate to take the nearest wood when in want of fuel to cook a meal. Houses inhabited by workmen who own them do not cost half as much for repairs as those tenanted in the ordinary way. In the third place, there can be no rack-renting.   Under such a system we could hear nothing of the 35 and even 50 per cent.

profits of grasping landlords. The workman sits rent free. And, in the fourth place, the man who owns his own house is in such a position of independence, comfort, and security as a tenant can never attain to. His house is then indeed his castle, into which no arbitrary landlord nor his emissaries with imperious summons to quit may enter. A comfortable house of his own (with a neat garden attached, if in the country) should be one of the first objects of the ambition of every working-man. The houses of Great Britain are divided into five classes, viz. :—

| Class | Homes. Thousands | Rental, Millions | Average Rental | Ratio of Houses | Va'ue, Millions |
|---|---|---|---|---|---|
| | | £ | £ | | £ |
| 1 | 21 | 14·0 | 665 | 0·4 | 280 |
| 2 | 238 | 28·5 | 120 | 4·3 | 570 |
| 3 | 512 | 17·9 | 35 | 9·3 | 358 |
| 4 | 1,294 | 19·4 | 15 | 23·4 | 388 |
| 5 | 3,410 | 34·4 | 10 | 62·6 | 688 |
| Total | 5,475 | 114·2 | 21 | 100·0 | 2,284 |

From this table you will see that the total value of the houses occupied by the working classes is above 688 million sterling, the annual rental of which is about 34 millions. ' Increase in the value of property rises from 50 to 70 millions sterling per annum—that is, on an average, 35 per cent. of the increase of national wealth. It is not merely the number of houses growing faster than population, but also a higher ratio of those paying house-duty. The average value per house in Great Britain has risen from 216l. in 1851 to 380l. in 1881 ; this is not including Ireland.' You will observe that work-men's houses constitute very nearly a third of the whole, and that consequently the increase in the value of this class of property erected every year will be nearly 20 millions sterling. If the workmen set themselves resolutely to the task of ac-quiring at least all their new houses, the whole would gradually pass into their possession, and what a magnificent and solid basis of property these houses, representing nearly one-twelfth of the entire property of the United Kingdom, would afford to the working classes who inhabit them ! The advantages, material and moral, which would accrue to themselves and to the State would be incalculable, and would afford scope for the

H

improvement, not merely of the present owners, but of generations yet unborn.  But how are you to acquire this property ?
Some of you will say : 'How can we get money to purchase
one tithe of it ?  Many of us have small wages and large
families, and it is a very easy thing to tell us to become the
owners of our own dwellings, but a very difficult thing to accomplish it.  Like many other Utopian schemes put forward
by social scientists, it looks very plausible, but, we are afraid,
is very impracticable.'  Well, I will show you the fund from
which you can pay for this gigantic property, by taking from
which, instead of curtailing your resources otherwise, you will
augment them a hundredfold.  It is out of the great drink
fund that you can so easily, and altogether beneficially, take
what in a very short time would make you possessors, not only
of all your dwelling-houses, but of a great deal more property
besides.  Now, I know that I am speaking to an exceptionally
intelligent audience and temperate section of working-men
(the convivial souls generally keep away from such lectures),
and you must understand that my remarks are not personal
but general, and refer altogether to averages.  The class in
Renton who would most benefit by my remarks is not here,
but you are mingling with them every day, and can easily dis-
seminate the gist of them.  I do not intend to give you a tee-
total lecture, but in any consideration of the subject before us
the enormous expenditure by the working classes upon drink and
tobacco will obtrude itself, and cannot be shut out.  To restate
the gist of what has been so largely dwelt upon in the chapter
on 'Popular Luxuries,' 'we shall be considerably within the
mark in assuming that the direct and indirect cost to the
nation arising from the use of intoxicating liquors cannot be
less than 200,000,000l. yearly.'  But we will leave out the cor-
relative waste, and take as nearly as possible the actual expenditure upon drink and tobacco.  Mr. Leone Levi, who went most
exhaustively into the statistics of the liquor traffic, calculated
the proportion consumed by the working classes at two-thirds
of the whole, and he calculated that a working-man with 36s. per
week, or 93l. per annum, expends about 40l. for food, 8l. for
house-rent, 25l. for fire, lighting, clothing, education, health,
and recreation, and 20l. for luxury, including 17l. 10s. for drink
and tobacco, including the taxes thereon.  The expenditure
upon alcohol is, I am very happy to say, falling off, and though
the average income of the workman has considerably increased
since Mr. Leone Levi's computation, yet his consumption of

drink has diminished. The expenditure upon drink in 1881 per inhabitant was about 2*l*. 16*s*. 5*d*., and of tobacco about 8*s*.; so that we may take 14*l*. per family per annum as a very safe under-estimate—I think about 30 per cent. under. There is a great diversity of opinion as to total abstinence, but none at all as to temperance. 1 think that every one of you will concur with me that the saving of at least half of the amount expended upon these luxuries, for the laudable object of securing the proprietorship of your own houses, would be an unalloyed benefit. There are about 5,600,000 working-class families in the country, and a saving of. 7*l*. per family would give the splendid total of 40,000,000*l*. sterling, which would serve to erect all the new houses which are being built for them, and leave 20,000,000*l*. over for the purchase of those already built. By a steady and general adoption of this principle the next generation of working-men would be living almost entirely in their own houses.

Having shown you how the funds are to be obtained, we have now to consider the best means of applying them. And I think there is no doubt that you can apply them to most advantage on the co-operative principle, by means of building societies. The advantages of a building society are that it collects its funds from members entirely upon the instalment system, and in such weekly sums as are convenient for all. It pays interest at the rate of 5 per cent. per annum on what is paid in—a better rate of interest than you could obtain in the savings-bank. Plans and title-deeds, in connection with property acquired by its members, are not only made out at less cost, but in a more thorough manner. Another very important advantage which it offers to the working-man is, that when he has accumulated a portion of the funds necessary for the erection of his house, he can get the balance advanced to him, and pay it up by instalments, thus securing entry very much earlier than if relying on his own resources. To give an example from the late Dr. Begg's experience, who was a great enthusiast in promoting building societies :—' Two young men of equal income occupy houses of equal value : the one is a member of the company, the other is not. The member of the company holds four shares ; the yearly rent of his house is 8*l*., and his landlord offers to sell it to him for 100*l*. Well, then, the company would advance this sum, and for the accommodation he would have to pay, by fortnightly instalments, the sum of 10*l*. 4*s*. per year. What is thereby his position ? Certainly something better than when he was a tenant paying 8*l.* a year to the landlord; he is now gradually, and, no doubt, very agreeably, undergoing a change which will leave him landlord. And what extra expenditure has he to make in attaining this? It is not 8*l.* or 10*l.* 4*s.* a year, but it is only the difference between these two sums, viz. 2*l.* 4*s.*, and that only till the house becomes his own, which will be the case in thirteen or fourteen years. Now, what is the other young man doing all the time? Why, he has also determined to be his own landlord, and he has adopted the method of in the meantime paying his rent, 8*l.* a year, and waiting till he can accumulate 100*l.* by depositing in the bank the amount of his saving, viz. 2*l.* 4*s.* a year. How long will he take to gain his object, even with the advantage of 3 per cent. compound interest added to his deposit? Will he do it in fourteen years? No, it will take thirty years. Which, then, is the more prudent of the two? Is it not evident that the one is certain of accomplishing in fourteen years what the other cannot accomplish in less than thirty years? But the loss of sixteen years is not all his folly, for what is the member of our company doing in the latter sixteen years of the thirty? He has now no rent to pay, and is able to lodge, year by year, in the bank 10*l.* 4*s.* What is the result at the end of the thirty years? Why, he has not only a house worth 100*l.*, but he has also in cash no less a sum than 200*l.* In short, the one has as the fruit of his thirty years' savings 300*l.*, the other 100*l.*' The worthy doctor's example in favour of the young man in the building society is, as is generally the case with men who enthusiastically take up any question, somewhat one-sided, no allowance having been made for depreciation and repairs; still, making all deductions, it shows very strongly the advantages of the co-operative system in this matter also, and it is to advise you all who do not own your own houses to enter such a society that is one of the principal objects of this lecture. I have been speaking hitherto as to what you should do in the way of acquiring property; but I have no doubt you would like to know very well what the Renton working-men have already done in this direction, and it is very necessary to know this before advising them further. I have been supplied with statistics on this point by Mr. Miller and Mr. Alex. Bayne, and others, which will interest you, and I am very much obliged to those gentlemen for the interest and trouble they have taken in this matter. I need scarcely state that there has been no prying curiosity as to individuals, but simply investigation as to general facts. Of the seven societies in Renton four collect and distribute funds. The Shepherds' Society, with a membership of 294, dispenses about 380*l.* per annum ; the Friendly, with a membership of 187, about 240*l.* ; the Oddfellows, with 60 members, about 100*l.* ; and the Sons of Temperance, with 62 members, about 50*l.*—in, all about 800*l.* per annum, to support their members in times of sickness —a most admirable provision—whilst they have of accumulated funds about 550*l.* In the Vale of Leven Savings Bank the Renton depositors have altogether 2,000*l.* ; in the Post Office Savings Bank, 250*l.* ; and in the Renton Penny Bank, 100*l.* In the Vale of Leven Co-operative Society there are 240 Renton members, with the very satisfactory sum of 5,340*l.* —a sum which, I think, will surprise you, and which I myself was very pleased to learn. Renton is exceptionally well served by its shopkeepers, many of whom are of a very high class indeed, and those who deal in this channel have no cause to complain, but on the contrary ; yet, for the sake of the business training which this co-operative movement insures, and the habits of thrift which it begets, and the better things in productive co-operation to which it is leading up, I must accord it my hearty sympathy, and advise the working-men of Renton to swell its ranks. The very study of its balance-sheets, which are put into the hands of each member every quarter, entirely superintended by working-men, who evidence the abilities of trained accountants, is a business education in itself, and must make him feel that he is a partner in a very large and well-managed business concern. And now, regarding house property. This very hall in which we are now located is possessed by the working-men of Renton to the extent of 610*l.* In the Vale of Leven and District Building Society there are 34 Renton members, with a capital in the society of 1,735*l.*, and a borrowed capital of 2,250*l.* In Renton there are 919 separate families, comprising 2,090 males and 2,644 females (you will observe that the female sex predominates here even much more than in other parts of the country), living in 896 houses, of which about 300 are of one apartment, 450 of two apartments, and the remainder of four apartments and upwards, the total value of which is about 120,000*l.* (at the moderate computation of fifteen years' purchase upon their assessable valuation), owned by 126 proprietors. I think you will be as much surprised as I was to learn that of these pro-

prietors 51, or about five-twelfths, are working-men, possessing property to the value of rather more than 30,000*l.*, being
one-fourth of the whole, and this is a most creditable state of
affairs for Renton. The total capital belonging to the working-men of Renton in local investments is about 40,000*l.*, and
there must be a good deal more privately invested outside of
the district. And now for a comparison of the Rentonians
with the country in general, in respect to their property. In
the matter of house property owned by working people—apart
from building societies—we have no national statistics, but I
think that the comparison would be very favourable for Renton.
In co-operative societies nearly a fourth of the working-class
families are interested throughout the country, with an average
of about 7*l.* per family ; in Renton about the same proportion
are members, but the average holding per family is about 22*l.*,
and here again Renton comes out very well. But in their
deposits in the savings-bank, in the accumulated funds of their
friendly societies, and in their investments in the building
society, the Rentonians compare very badly. Throughout the
country generally, the deposits in savings-banks amount to
about 45*s.* per inhabitant. In Glasgow they are as high as
140*s.* ; but in Renton only 8*s.* 6*d.* In friendly and provident
societies throughout the country there is a little over a fourth
of the working population enrolled, with an accumulated
capital of nearly 4*l.* per member ; in Renton there is only
about one-eighth and with accumulated capital of under 1*l.*
per member. I was disappointed when I made this comparison, for I thought Renton would come out well in the matter
of friendly societies. One great cause of regret in some of
our friendly societies has been, that they have made it almost
their exclusive aim to provide against temporary sickness.
The building up of a solid platform of property in youth and
middle age, on which they might serenely and comfortably
rest in old age, has unfortunately been beyond their scope. In
the country generally there are about 2 per cent. of the population enrolled as members of building societies, with a capital
of about 100*l.* per member ; but in Renton there are scarcely
three-quarters per cent., with only about 50*l.* per member.
The general result of the comparison is, that while a picked
body of the working-men in Renton, comprising 240 co-operators and 51 landlords, compare favourably with the average
throughout the country, the great mass of the Rentonians
are very far behind. I must give the Renton co-operators and

working-class landlords much credit for the wisdom displayed by them in their investments.

I was one of the Executive in connection with the recent Sanitary Congress, held in Glasgow, and took a good deal of interest in its proceedings, and was present at the meeting of working-men in St. Andrew's Hall, to hear Dr. Carpenter, the distinguished sanitarian. The Lord Provost, who presided, pointed with pride to the three and a half millions of deposits in the Glasgow savings-banks, but the lecturer took occasion to remark that he considered that a large portion of this would be better invested in the proper housing of its owners. While by no means seeking to disparage the system of depositing in savings-banks and friendly societies, I think that working people's savings can be much more profitably invested in their own dwelling-houses and co-operative societies, and are just as available in the time of need. In Lancashire alone no less than 134,783l. was withdrawn from the funds of building and other co-operative societies during 1862, the year of greatest distress. But to people who can save only in very small instalments, the savings-bank, and especially your well-managed Penny Savings Bank, are of inestimable value, and all young people, with small wages, should begin in it, and progress to the better things which I have shown you. Thrift needs only a beginning. One of the Glasgow magistrates, to whom I was speaking of the subject of this lecture, told me of a servant of his who dressed so extravagantly that she was always in debt. His sister often remonstrated with her without effect. At last, as an expedient, she deposited half a sovereign in the savings-bank for the girl, and gave her the bank-book. In the course of a year or so his sister had again to remonstrate with her, but this time for a very different reason—for not dressing respectably enough. She had taken too eagerly to the depositing of all her money in the savings-bank. Trade in Renton has, on the whole, been very steady, and there is no reason why there should not be a great improvement in the means held by working people. Mrs. Graham and others, who have had experience of the slums in our great cities, can tell you that there is no such abject poverty here. In London and other large cities there are vast colonies, compared with which this village would form but a drop in the bucket, living in a manner far more wretched than our poorest. But that there is very much room for improvement in the mode of living of many of the people in Renton, I do not need to tell

you.  A manufacturer, who was here on business on Thursday
last, remarked that he had never seen such a dirty place—not
even in the worst slums of Manchester.  There is, unfortunately, a large number of houses of a most unsatisfactory
description, tenanted principally by the very large proportion
of the Irish population who have taken up their residence
amongst us, and who have to be educated up to a higher
standard of house accommodation than they have been accustomed to in their own country ; the average value of house
property, per inhabitant, in Ireland, being 12*l.*, and in Scotland 60*l.*  The Irishman has many good points about him, and
has been sent amongst us for his better training, and the School
Board, and other agencies, are aiding us very much in advancing
his cultivation.  The class of houses in Renton has of late very
much improved, and there is no reason why we should not have
it a model village in a very short time.  Assuming that the
Rentonians consume the average amount of spirits and tobacco
(and I am afraid they are quite up to the standard in this
respect), there must be an expenditure of about 20,000*l.* per
annum on these two items alone, but to be quite safe let us put
it down at 13,000*l.*  Now, if you choose to curtail this expenditure by a half, you have the princely sum of 6,500*l.* to expend
every year on the general improvement of your style of living,
and principally, I should advise, in your style of housing.  By
paying into the Vale of Leven Building Society, say, 5,000*l.* a
year, leaving your 1,500*l.* for other worthy objects, and getting
it judiciously expended in the pulling down of old and erection
of new and comfortable dwellings, you would soon effect such
a transformation in the appearance and condition of our village
as would render it one of the finest in the country.  Its natural
situation is admirable, and its present construction offers no
insuperable obstacles to a thorough renovation.  In many of
the leading industries of the country there occur floods of
prosperity, in which the workmen engaged in them reap very
high wages.  These, you would say, are halcyon days for the
workpeople to accumulate some of the extra money passing
through their hands.  Such a flood of prosperity has within the
last two or three years been the good fortune of the iron
trade, and especially those branches of it connected with shipbuilding.  Dumbarton, as you know, is a great seat of this
industry, and many of the Dumbarton workmen live in Renton.
The riveters are the class of workers who have reaped the
highest wages in this good trade.  What good has it done

them ?   There are, no doubt, a few who have made good use
of their means, but the great majority have spent them in riot
and debauchery, many families, earning five and even as much
as ten pounds per week, living in houses of the most abject
description, and with literally no furniture, save one or two
indispensable articles.   The deposits of these highly-paid men
in the savings-bank are most meagre, and this fact, in connection with the same class of workmen in Govan, has been the
subject of comment in the Glasgow papers.   They work only
two-thirds of their time, keeping back all their more sober and
industrious fellow-workmen.   A Roman Catholic priest, whose
charge was in Dumbarton during the previous high-pressure
in trade, told a friend of mine that women often called upon
him on the Monday mornings begging, whose husbands had, on
the previous Saturdays, lifted 14*l.* to 20*l.* as their fortnight's
pay—'a rate of remuneration which' (the worthy father added
pathetically) 'I have never had myself, nor ever will have.'
The most of you will remember a precisely similar state of
affairs when the colliers had their turn.   When Mr. Smiles
visited Renfrewshire a few years ago, the colliers were earning
from ten to fourteen shillings a day.   According to the common
saying, they were 'making money like a minting-machine.'   To
take an instance :—'A father and three sons were earning sixty
pounds a month, or equal to a united income of more than
seven hundred pounds a year.   The father was a sober, steady
man.   While the high wages lasted, he was the first to enter
the pit in the morning, and the last to leave it at night.   He
only lost five days in one year (1873–4), the loss being occa-
sioned by fast-days and holidays.   Believing that the period
of high wages could not last long, he and his sons worked as
hard as they could.   They saved a good deal of money, and
bought several houses, besides educating themselves to occupy
higher positions.   In the same neighbourhood another collier,
with four sons, was earning money at about the same rate per
man—that is, about seventy-five pounds per month, or nine
hundred pounds a year.   This family bought five houses within
a year, and saved a considerable sum besides.   The last information we had respecting them was that the father had
become a contractor, that he employed about sixty colliers and
" reddsmen," and was allowed so much for every ton of coals
brought to bank.   The sons were looking after their father's
interests.   They were all sober, diligent, sensible men, and
took a great deal of interest in the education and improvement

of the people in their neighbourhood. At the same time that
these two families of colliers were doing so well, it was very
different with the majority of their fellow-workmen. These only
worked for about three days in every week. Some spent their
earnings in the public-house ; others took a whisky "ploy" at
the sea-side. For that purpose they hired all the gigs,
droskies, cabs, or "machines" about a fortnight beforehand.
The results were seen as the successive Monday mornings came
round. The magistrate sat in the neighbouring town, where
a number of men and women, with black eyes and broken
heads, were brought before him for judgment. Before the
time of high wages the court-house business was got through
in an hour—sometimes there was no business at all. But
when the wages were doubled, the magistrate could scarcely
get through the business in a day. It seemed as if high wages
meant more idleness, more whisky, and more broken heads
and faces.' No State provision, neither any help from landowner or employer, could do workmen such as these any good in
the way of providing them with better house accommodation.
Let every workman who has the golden opportunity of big
wages resulting from pressure of trade take advantage of it to
store up something for the rainy day, which, he may be quite
certain, is not far distant. But even with very moderate
wages, if proper thrift be exercised, it is quite within the
means of the ordinary working-man to provide the where-
withal to purchase a comfortable dwelling for himself and
family. I have just been looking particularly at a house
which is being built and now nearly finished, overlooking the
Cordale grounds—I refer to the one owned by your worthy
fellow-workman, Daniel M'Gregor. It is well and substan-
tially built, and has a very ornamental appearance, good out-
houses attached, and a nice piece of garden-ground. The
total cost, he informs me, will be about 450l., and will give a
but and a ben to four separate families, which is equal to
about 112l. for house accommodation for a family. It is quite
common for the members of building societies to join their
means for the sake of economy in the erection of a joint house
—indeed, there is another house quite close to this one owned
by two workmen. If you join the Vale of Leven Building
Society, and take, say, five shares, which would give you an
ample margin, whenever you have got about 6l. paid up, the
society would advance you the balance, for which you would
pay 5l. per annum of interest, and go on paying up the

balance of your shares, which may be made at the rate of 6*d*. per share per week, or more, as may be arranged, and in the course of ten to fifteen years each home would be your own property. A better plan still is for the frugal bachelor and thrifty spinster to begin their instalments several years before matrimony, and settle down in a comfortably furnished house of their own. Many a lad at the works begins to earn about a pound per week at eighteen years of age. Out of this he could often without hardship put 4*s*. per week into the building society, and at the age of twenty-eight be able to settle down with a partner for life, who might also have had a little laid past for the furniture, in a house of their own, and never require to pay one penny for rent during the whole of their married life. What an advantage to a working-man with a young family this would be, those parents best know who have the landlord or factor appearing regularly at Whitsuntide and Martinmas with his hand out for four or five pounds of their hard earned and sorely needed money. For people of better means the house to which I have referred, divided into halves, would give first-rate accommodation for two families, and for well-to-do tradesmen with grown-up families, also earning good wages, it would serve capitally as a self-contained villa. In our own works at the present time there are nearly 100 families earning 100*l*. per annum and upwards, and there must be a considerable proportion of Dumbarton workers who reside in Renton who do the same. Thirty-four members from Renton in the building society is a very small number. I trust that one of the results of this lecture will be a very great increase in this number. And now for more immediately practical advice. I would like as many of our foremen and others earning good wages as possible to join the Vale of Leven and District Building Society, and if you set about it in earnest, and show the proprietor of the land by your numbers that it would be really worth his while, I have no doubt he would be very pleased to feu off portions of ground on a plan suited for superior houses, on which to erect comfortable and beautiful dwellings in advantageous proximity to each of the works, and form such convenient and pleasant houses your own property, as would cause you to look back with amazement at the tumble-down and dirt-begirt tenements for which many of you are content at present to pay such high rents, as, judiciously expended in this society, would in the course of a few years defray the cost of becoming your own landlords. If this scheme be taken up, as I trust it will, by a sufficient number, I would be very glad to do anything for you in my power. For the sake of your own health and that of your children, for the sake of your independence, but above all for the sake of your moral welfare, I advise you to look to the matter of property, and first of all to the acquisition of your own dwellings. The whole question of the acquisition of property by the working classes is at the root of it, and principally a moral one, and your ministers, your Sabbath-school teachers, and your fellow-workmen of consistent Christian example, and all who are helping to elevate the moral tone of the community, are also helping more strongly than any other means to solve satisfactorily the question of the division of property amongst the different classes of the people, and to improve their physical condition. All honour to those brave souls who go nobly into the fight against the moral evils of society. Most assuredly in the wake of their efforts will follow greater material prosperity. At the beginning of the lecture I quoted from our national poet lines speaking contemptuously of property, and I will conclude by an extract from an epistle also written by him, addressed to Andrew Aiken, the son of his old friend, Robert Aiken, writer, Ayr, a young man who afterwards earned distinction in the service of his country, and giving him admirable advice—

> To ca'ch Dame Fortune's golden smile,
> Assiduous wait upon her ;
> And gather gear by every wile
> That's justified by honour ;
> Not for to hide it in a hedge,
> Not for a train attendant,
> But for the glorious privilege
> Of being independent.

# CONCLUSION.

THE great towering economical phenomenon of the nineteenth century, eclipsing in its results everything of the same kind in ancient history, and overshadowing all that have occurred in more modern times, has been the sudden, easy, and most advantageous acquisition by this country of a labour saving and productive power equal to more than the united strength of a hundred millions of men, by means of the steam engine and other contemporaneous inventions. This has been, as it were, an enormous gift of the means of life put into the people's hands, exceeding by far in yearly value the rent of land, or even of land and houses combined; and surely, if any accession of merely material wealth could have raised them to the lofty position which many theorisers consider sure to follow upon the equal distribution of property, or (as some of the less sweeping reformers think) of the land alone, this large and altogether unprecedented good fortune would not have failed to secure it. But we cannot shut our eyes to the evils and defects which still abound in our social system. To publish as a panacea for these an increase of the material resources of the country, or a forced redistribution of the whole or a portion of those already existing, by simple legislative enactment, is short-sighted, foolish, and mischievous.

As the people advance in intelligence and morality, legislation should advance along with them. Severe enactments necessary for a debased and ignorant populace can be modified, or even altogether dispensed with, amongst one more moral and intelligent, and liberal measures introduced, the administration of which would have formerly been impracticable. I trust that all needful improvement in our laws may not be found lagging behind, but keeping pace with the times.

But legislation (to which I have not much referred in these chapters, as being outside of their intended scope) occupies a very subordinate position amongst the ameliorating agencies, as compared with the industry, economy, intelligence, and morality of the people, and upon these I have insisted as the principal means of national advancement, and without which all else is valueless.

There has been progress ; we are progressing in the path of economical, physical, and moral improvement. The task of the social reformer of to-day in accelerating this progress is an easier and a happier one than that of many who have had to stem their country's backward course, and should be entered upon earnestly and hopefully.

My own views as to our present economic condition, and to the immediate steps to be taken in still further improving it, are embodied in these preceding chapters, and may be summed up in a few words :—

*Labour*, the law of man's life, forced upon him by his physical necessities, and, under whatever name known, the only means of human pleasure and improvement, yet requiring to be wisely regulated, so that there may be no luxurious sloth on the one hand nor injurious overwork on the other—is still in this country, in many cases, pursued in a manner contrary to all the laws of human physiology. The very first object to which our recent great accession of labour saving and productive power should be applied is to abolish all over-exertion in our industries, and to make all labour sweet and wholesome.

*Leisure* (if such it can properly be called)—cold, hunger-bitten, dreary, and monotonous—is possessed by the savages of Arctic regions during the greater part of the year ; leisure—listless, lazy, and apathetic—by those in tropical climes ; and leisure—indolent, debauched, and luxurious—for short periods by our intemperate workmen. The leisure of civilisation proper—learned and refined, the fruit of and braced up to vigorous enjoyment by manly, active work—has hitherto fallen t. the lot of only small sections of the human race. The second object to which our enormous scientific power should be applied is to introduce more and more of pleasant and healthful leisure amongst our working classes—firstly, for their children, to give them better education ; secondly, for their wives and daughters, to insure a better domestic economy ; and, thirdly, for themselves in times of sickness and in the decline of life ; but until these conditions of prime importance have been attained, and until the pressure of foreign competition has been relaxed by reduction of its working hours nearer to our own, our working-men should not seek to reduce their own hours of labour below those now prescribed by law for women and young persons.]

*Luxury* holds a very important position amongst the civilising agencies, and forms one of the most powerful incentives to industry, invention, and progress in the arts of life ; and the third object to which our great increase of material resources should be applied is to elevate the common standard of living, so that a great many beneficial things which are now luxuries should become necessaries. But an excessive use of luxuries, especially of some kinds, is productive of many evils. The use of luxuries by our working classes is enormous, and being the result of enfeebled morality, and inseparably allied with other cognate vices, is also a great cause of concentration of wealth, and consequently of the luxuries of wealth, so that luxuriousness is exactly proportionate to inequality in the possession of property. To elevate their standard of living they must acquire a larger share of property by saving that which is now expended upon vicious luxuries. *More temperate labour, greater leisure, and superior living must all rest upon the basis of a more extended possession of property. The broader the base the higher and nobler the structure which can be reared upon it. Indeed, the whole question of* LABOUR, LEISURE, AND LUXURY *(which is essentially one, though thus divided)—of labour, temperate and healthful, of peaceful and cultured leisure, and of luxury, pleasant and refined—in a word, of economic* PROGRESS *— is bound up in the question of* THE ACQUISITION OF PROPERTY BY THE WORKING CLASSES.

What property should first be acquired and how it is to be acquired I have attempted to show in the last chapter, and though inculcating upon our working-men to rely principally upon their own efforts, I would say to those who have more time and better education :—' Come over and help them to help themselves, for you can be of immense service to them.'

# APPENDICES.

## APPENDIX TO 'LABOUR.'

*Note* 1.

'The legality of keeping in children after school hours for non-preparation of home lessons is about to be tested in the Queen's Bench Division. Some Bradford people have faced the question thus far. A memorial, signed by above fifty medical men in that town, has just been presented to the local School Board, praying the Board to dispense with home lessons in the case of children under ten. It is said that inflammation of the brain among school children has increased by 50 per cent. since the current Education Acts came into force.'

'Dr. Forbes Winslow furnishes a contribution to the discussion on the subject of over-pressure in schools. He says he has been a witness to the injurious results of the present severe mental culture, and denounces the system of cramming for the purpose of obtaining the Government grant as being rotten at its very foundation. After asserting that many children become hopelessly demented, whilst others become unfitted for the serious duties of life in consequence of the strain laid upon them, Dr. Forbes Winslow remarks :—" The question is one of such great importance throughout England, that the sympathy of humanity in general must be secured in the welfare of the children of our great nation." '

These quotations give the extreme opinion on the question.

*Note* 2.

The following is extracted from a letter from one of the girls in a fashionable millinery establishment in the West-End of London, which appeared in the *St. James's Gazette*, March 24, 1884 :—

'I don't know how it may be in some of the large places where a great number of young ladies are employed; but this is what it is at Mdme. Célimène's. We have to begin work at eight every morning; and we go on till eight at night, without any stopping except for our meals. We are supposed to have two hours for these; but

I

in the season, when we are all busy and have more orders than we can get through, we often don't have as much as an hour for all our meals together.  Of course that is against the law, as we all know, because a printed copy of the Factory Act hangs up on the wall of the work-room ; and we can't very well help seeing it, because it is the only ornament there, except some bundles of silk and thread and a good many fly-marks.  But it does not do us much good to know that the law is being broken one day in every two.  There is nobody to complain to except the inspector, and when he comes he generally walks round with Mdme. Célimène or the forewoman ; and of course any girl who said anything to him when they were by would lose her place directly, and perhaps never get another.  So we think it wiser to hold our tongues.  If we could let out all we knew, we could tell other ways in which the law is broken. -Perhaps you would not believe it, but it is true all the same, that in many a house of business the girls are kept working till half-past ten and eleven o'clock day after day through the best part of the season.  That may not seem very much, I dare say, when you hear it told ; but it is bad enough when you have to do it.  Where I am there are twenty girls—dressmakers and milliners—all sitting round three oblong tables in a room not bigger than an ordinary drawing-room, with only one window.  You can think what the air of that room is like in July when we have all been working in it for twelve hours.  There we sit all through the morning, afternoon, and evening—twenty of us—stitching and trimming away, with the sun pouring in on us, and the room getting closer and closer till you feel you can hardly bear it any longer ; and then, when eight o'clock comes, and you are dying to get out and have a mouthful of fresh air, you are told that you will have to stop for an hour longer, or perhaps two or three hours.  I have seen some of the younger girls put their heads down and cry quietly when they heard they could not go, and I have felt like crying myself, if it was any use.  Perhaps you won't believe this is the case, because you know it is illegal to keep us working more than twelve hours without a special order.  But I know that it is done sometimes ; and I dare say, if anybody was to inquire carefully, he would find that it is done very often.  Now and then it gets found out, and you hear of somebody being summoned and fined ; but it happens lots of times when it is not found out.  Of course the girls might tell the inspector ; but none of us would dare to say anything to him.  Besides Mdme. Célimène is a very nice lady with very nice manners, and when she says to the inspector that it is all right, of course he does not doubt her.

' But I think the work is too hard for us, even when they don't go beyond the proper time.  I think twelve hours' work every day except Saturday is too much for most women.  Lots of the girls are quite young, and some have been brought up in the country.  They come to be apprenticed looking as fresh and healthy as possible ; but after two or three years you would be surprised at the change in them. They have lost all their freshness and have grown thin and pale; and I could tell you of more than one that has faded away and gone into a decline through being at business too long. You have no idea how you feel at the end of the week when you have been sewing every minute, as you may say, and only stopping when you are asleep. Your head is swimming and your eyes hazy, and you can't sleep properly or enjoy your food. It is no wonder you get out of sorts; but of course most of us can't afford to indulge our fancies, and have to go on working whether we are quite up to it or not. It is just the two or three hours at the end that are the worst. If they ever make a new Factory Act, I hope they will make it the law that we are to work only nine hours or ten hours, instead of twelve. Women must work for their living often enough; but I don't think they ought to be allowed to work so hard that they ruin their health in a very few years. Besides, it is harder a great deal than most young men work, I am sure. My brother George is a clerk in a warehouse in the City, and he begins at nine and comes away at six; and then in summer he goes off to play cricket or rides his bicycle. Mother says George looks the picture of health, while I am getting thinner and paler every day; and what wonder?

'There is another thing that perhaps you don't know about young ladies in houses of business. I know that in some of the large houses, when the girls are not working they have plenty of ways of amusing themselves, because there are pianos for them, and reading-rooms with books and newspapers, and so on. But that is not the case with us in the better-class West-End places. The houses are generally rather small, and there is not any room to spare; and so it happens that very often there is no place for you to go to after your work is done but the hot and stuffy workroom, where you have been sitting all day, or perhaps the kitchen where you have had your supper. Well, of course it is not surprising that a good many of the girls run out into the street just to get a little air and to stretch themselves a bit. At Mdme. Célimène's you need not be indoors before eleven, and if you give the housemaid something she will let you stay out a bit later. Now, I dare say you will see that a lot of girls come to no good that way. And it is the same on Sunday. Mdme. Célimène lets us go away to our friends on Saturday if we like, and stop till Sunday evening. Some of us have got relations living in London, like me; and then of course we can go to them. But a good many have no friends in London; and if they do not manage to make acquaintances of some kind, there would be nothing for them to do all Sunday but to stop in the house; nowhere for them to go to but that workroom, and perhaps a close little attic bedroom that they share with one or two other girls. Many people are taking trouble now about seeing that working people get better lodgings and more time to amuse themselves. Of course the young ladies like me don't want anything done for us in the way of charity; but I do think that a little more care ought to be taken of us—about giving us shorter hours and more time to ourselves. I know work-girls who have got married, and have a whole family of miserable-looking children with no strength in them; and if the doctors knew how they had to live from the time that they were fifteen to the time that they were twenty or five-and-twenty, I dare say they wouldn't find it hard to tell the reason.'

### Note 3.

As to capacity for work, it is stated that the 'Germans do not get through so much work as Englishmen; ' but they are 'generally more docile, intelligent, and trustworthy than the English. They are temperate. Time-breaking through drink is almost unknown.' There is said to be nothing of the irregularity to be observed even among really good men in England.—*Report of Royal Commission on Technical Instruction.*

### Note 4.

The American captain was good company when one got over the brusqueness of his manner. He told me a singular thing. I had been looking at his crew, and had been puzzled to make out what they were, or how he had picked them up. 'I make a rule,' he said, 'when I engage my men for a voyage, to take no English, no Scotch, no Irish, no Americans. There is no getting along with them. They go a-shore in harbour, get drunk, get into prison, give me nothing but trouble. It is the same with them all, my people and yours equally.' 'Then whom do you take?' I asked in astonishment. 'I take Danes,' he answered; 'I take Norwegians, Germans, Swedes; all of these I can trust. They are sober, they make no row, are never in the hands of the police. They save their wages, are always quiet and respectable, and I know that I can depend on them. The firemen, ship's servants, &c., are Chinamen; I can trust them too.' I recollect a Portuguese nigger at the island of St. Vincent once showing me, with a grin, an iron-grated cage, and telling me it was specially reserved for English sailors. At the time I thought him a malicious lying rascal—one never knows about these things.—FROUDE'S *Oceana*, p. 203.

# APPENDIX TO 'LEISURE.'

## *Note* 1.

'The equivalent of one man's work on the great farms of Dakota is 5,500 bushels of wheat per annum, if the crop reach 20 bushels to the acre. Retaining enough for seed, this quantity suffices to make 1,000 barrels of flour. It can be carried through the flour-mill and put into barrels, including the labour of making the barrel, at the equivalent of one other man's labour for one year ; and at the ratio of the work done to each man employed upon the New York Central Railroad, the wheat can be moved from Dakota to a flour-mill in Minnesota, and thence the 1,000 barrels of flour can be moved to the city of New York, and all the machinery of the farm, the mill, and the railroad can be kept in repair at the equivalent of the labour of two more men ; so that 1,000 barrels of flour, the annual ration of 1,000 people, can be placed in the city of New York from a point 2,000 miles distant with the exertion of the human labour equivalent to that of only four men, working one year in producing, milling, and moving the wheat. It can there be baked and distributed by the work of three more persons ; so that seven persons serve 1,000 with bread.'

## *Note* 2.

'As regards the future, should any symptoms present themselves that foreign competition is becoming more effective in this respect, it must be for the country and the workman himself to decide whether the advantages of the shorter hours compensate for the increased cost of production or diminished output. We believe that they do, and on social as well as economical grounds we should regret to see any curtailment of the leisure and freedom which the workman now enjoys.

'No advantages which could be expected to accrue to the commerce of the country would in our opinion compensate for such a change.'—*Report of Commission on Depression of Trade*, Clause 82.

## *Note* 3.

*Youthful Development.*—In his guide to the physical examination and measurement of the human body, Mr. C. Roberts. F.R.C.S., says that the mean height attained, so far as his averages go, by the children of the higher professional families brought up in the country, at and over twenty-three years of age, is 68·86 inches, or 5 feet 8¾ inches. The corresponding weight is 152 pounds. Town-bred youth of the same class are 0·69 of an inch shorter ; 67·28 inches is the corresponding height attained by the children of shop-keepers, 67·10 inches by agricultural and other labourers, 66·77 inches by artisans, and only 64·87 inches by idiots and imbeciles. The corresponding weight of the latter unfortunate class is 123 pounds. The American boy of eighteen attains a height of 67·44 inches and a weight of 138 pounds in selected schools, and 66·76 inches in height and 115 pounds in weight in public schools, against 68·29 inches in height and 146 pounds in weight of the English public-school boy. Thus the effect of higher mental training, when accompanied by suitable food and healthy surroundings generally, seems to tend rather to the development than to the stunting of the physical energies of youth.

*Note 4.*

The statistical aspect of this question of employment of women may be appropriately concluded by the presentation of the following summary of the total number of females employed in industrial occupations, relatively to the total number of both sexes so employed in the principal countries of the world :—

|  | Total Industrial Workers | Of which there are Females | Percentage Proportion of Females |
|---|---|---|---|
| United Kingdom . . . . | 7,997,529 | 2,005,304 | 25 |
| United States . . . . . | 3,837,112 | 631,079 | 16 |
| France . . . . . . . | 4,465,000 | 1,565,000 | 35 |
| Prussia . . . . . . . | 3,650,000 | 583,000 | 16 |
| Austria . . . . . . . | 2,279,000 | 964,500 | 42 |

The facts and figures that have been collated in this chapter speak for themselves. They show that England occupies an intermediate position between the United States and the Continent of Europe, in reference to the numbers of women employed in industrial occupations.—JEANS' *England's Supremacy*, p. 356.

*Note 5.*

The development of industrial companies has taken place at a rate which has quite outpaced the progress of the other life companies. The Prudential has continued to show a great increase in its membership; but there is no room in such an enormous organisation for the ratio of expansion that has taken place in one or two other companies. The Pearl, the Refuge, the British Workman's, and other industrial companies, as well as the largest of the collecting friendly societies—the Royal Liver, the Royal London, and the Liverpool Victoria Legal—have shown additions to the number of their members and amount of their premium income, great in themselves and quite astonishing in comparison with their previous returns.—*The Insurance Directory and Year Book*, 1886, p. 2.

# APPENDIX TO 'LUXURY.'

## Note 1.

### Statistics for 1870.

Population of United Kingdom . . . 30,000,000
Number of manual labour class . . . 22,000,000
Middle and higher classes . . . . 8,000,000
Total National Income . . . . . £953,420,902
Manual labour class income . . . . £418,000,000
Giving 19*l.* per head, or 85*l.* per family.
Average earning of working class family per week 33*s.*

Real and personal property of United Kingdom . £6,000,000,000
Working class proportion . . . . . . £300,000,000
Giving 14*l.* per head, or 60*l.* per family.

Upper class proportion 5,700,000,000*l.*, being upwards of 700*l.* per head, or about 3,200*l.* per family.
Gross number of persons with incomes of 200*l.* and upwards 450,000.
Aggregate income of same 400,000,000*l.*

## Division of Income.

. £140,000,000 appropriated by 9,000 persons.
110,000,000 ,, ,, 55,000 ,,
150,000,000 ,, ,, 336,000 ,,

Schedule A.
In respect of lands, tenements, &c. . . . . £133,478,032

Schedule B.
In respect of the occupation of lands . . . 37,447,774

Schedule C.
In respect of annuities, dividends, &c. . . . 34,790,120

Schedule D.
In respect of professions, trades, employments, railways, mines, ironworks, &c. . . . . 161,594,118

Schedule E.
In respect of public offices . . . . . 22,110,858
                                              —————————
                                              £389,420,902

Unreturned profits under Schedule D.　.　.　45,000,000
The 60*l.* a year excused to incomes between 100*l.* and
200*l.*　.　.　.　.　.　.　.　.　.　.　15,000,000
Incomes not charged to Income Tax .　.　.　.　86,000,000

Total income of upper classes　.　.　. £535,420,902

Income of manual labour classes estimated by Mr.
Levi　.　.　.　.　.　.　.　.　.　. 418,000,000

Total National Income.　.　.　.　. £953,420,000

Upper and middle class expenditure for luxuries, 370,000,000*l.*
Rent of land of the 133,000,000*l.* in Schedule A = 60,000,000*l.*
Amount used for the luxury of the upper classes, 35,000,000*l.*
Game licences, 49,802.
Gamekeepers, 4,584.
Dwelling-houses over 20*l.*, 450,679 = 23,267,149*l.* value.
Luxurious expenditure in houses, 20,000,000*l.*

In respect of the luxurious occupation and application
of the land　.　.　.　.　.　.　.　. £35,000,000
In respect of the luxurious occupation of dwelling-
houses　.　.　.　.　.　.　.　.　.　. 20,000,000
In respect of the luxurious application of railways,
mines, iron works, and all other capital except lands
and tenements; also of the services of those, other
than the working classes, engaged in professions,
trades, employments, public offices, &c. .　.　. £100,000,000

In all　.　.　. £155,000,000

## *Workers for Luxury.*

| | Persons | Wages |
|---|---|---|
| Domestic Servants (the whole)　.　. | 1,693,200 | £59,000,000 |
| Messengers and Porters (two-thirds)　. | 64,000 | 1,730,000 |
| Builders and Labourers (a third) .　. | 263,000 | 15,733,000 |
| Cabinet-makers and Upholsterers (two-thirds)　.　.　.　.　.　.. | 33,000 | 2,120,000 |
| Coachmakers (two-thirds)　.　.　. | 16,000 | 920,000 |
| Wood Carvers (the whole)　.　.　. | 24,000 | 1,500,000 |
| Silk Manufacturers (two-thirds)　.　. | 80,000 | 1,680,000 |
| Hosiery and Lace (a third)　.　.　. | 75,000 | 2,220,000 |
| Hairdressers (two-thirds)　.　.　. | 7,000 | 460,000 |
| Glove Manufacturers (five-sixths) .　. | 20,000 | 750,000 |
| Leather Case Manufacturers (the whole) | 4,800 | 320,000 |
| Gold, Silver, &c., Manufacturers (nine-tenths)　.　.　.　.　.　. | 20,000 | 1,500,000 |
| | 2,300,000 | £87,933,000 |

Workers of all other classes . . . 3,210,000     127,067,000

Total Workers for the Luxuries of Wealth . . . . . . 5,510,000     £215,000,000

Amount paid to manual labour class for producing and maintaining luxuries, 215,000,000*l.*

Tax on tea and coffee . . . . . . . £9,470,000
Tax on alcoholic liquors and tobacco . . . . 29,126,000
Total taxes on stimulants . . . . . . 38,690,000

Tax per head on gross income in United Kingdom 10*d.* per pound.

### Note 2.

Assuming the working classes to comprise seventy per cent. of the population, and with small farmers, crofters, and others to number 26,000,000 persons, or 5,600,000 families, the 12,200,000 workers give 2·17 earners for every family.

The number of persons to a family was, in 1881, 4·61 in England and Wales, 4·63 in Scotland, and 5·19 in Ireland, giving an average for the United Kingdom of 4·67 persons to a family.

### Note 3.

*Estimates of Total Income of United Kingdom.*

|  | Mu'hall 1883 | Levi 1879–80 | Giffen 1883 | Our Own 1884 |
|---|---|---|---|---|
|  | £ | £ | £ | £ |
| Income-Tax payers . | 574,000,000 | 577,000,000 | 602,000,000 | 641,129,500 |
| Incomes not charged to Income-Tax . | 244,000,000 | 143,000,000 | 118,000,000 | 180,000,000 |
| Working class income | 447,000,000 | 1884 521,000,000 | 550,000,000 | 521,000,000 |
| Total. . . . | 1,265,000,000 | 1,241,000,000 | 1,270,000,000 | 1,342,129,500 |

Giffen gives 602,000,000*l.* as the estimate for the income-tax payers, but in this I presume he has added only 16 per cent. for unreturned profits, which would give an amount of about 40,000,000*l.* following the same estimate as Mr. Dudley Baxter, whereas judging from the Reports of the Income-Tax Commissioners it amounts to about 35 per cent., which gives 90,000,000*l.* I have, however, deducted from this sum 20,000,000*l.* for possible overcharges, leaving 70,000,000*l.* to be added for unreturned profits under Schedule D, and making the total incomes charged to income-tax 641,000,000*l.*

Mr. Giffen, however, has a strong impression that a much larger figure than his own might be taken.

In *The Report of the Commissioners of Inland Revenue* (1870, vol. i. p. 130–131), referring to the large evasions practised under

Schedule D by means of fraudulent returns, they state that some
years ago they received 11,000*l.* from one person, and in 1865 10,500*l.*
from another, for duty on income which had not been returned for
assessment. The latter payment represented an income of 13,000*l.*
a year from the imposition of the tax in 1842 to April 1865. On
examination of the claims for compensation put forward with recent
metropolitan improvements, it was found that 40 per cent. of the
persons assessed had understated their incomes to such an extent
that a true return would give 130 per cent. more than they had paid.
The Commissioners are of opinion that this may be taken as giving
a rough approximation of the extent to which the revenue is de-
frauded under Schedule D. They state that they have found every
class of contributors to Schedule D liable to the same shortcomings in
their returns, not excepting public companies and large joint-stock
associations, and estimate at 57,000,000*l.* the entire sum on which
duty was evaded, and ' they see no reason to distrust this estimate—at
all events, no reason to consider that it errs on the side of excess
rather than otherwise.'

*Note 4.*

Lady Manners, in a recent number of the *National Review*, gives
an account of ' The Life of Luxury and Self-indulgence ' which prevails when parties are entertained in well-appointed sporting country
houses in England or in shooting lodges in Scotland, from which
the following is extracted :—' Before the ladies—indeed, before most
of the gentlemen—leave their beds dainty little services of tea and
bread and butter are carried to them. Sometimes the younger men
prefer brandy and soda. Fortified by these refreshments, the non-
sporting guests come to breakfast about ten. Four hot dishes, every
sort of cold meat that might fitly furnish forth a feast, fruits, cake,
tea, coffee, cocoa, claret on the sideboard, constitute a satisfactory
breakfast, often prolonged till within two hours and a half of
luncheon. The important institution of luncheon begins at two.
Again the table is spread with many varieties of flesh and fowl, hot
and cold proofs of the cook's ability, plum puddings for those who
study their health, and creations in cream for those who have not
yet devoted themselves to that never-failing source of influence.
Coffee is served after lunch, which is usually over soon after three.
The ladies gather round the tea-table about five, usually showing
much appreciation of any little surprises in the way of muffins or
tea-cakes provided by a thoughtful mistress. At eight or half-past
dinner will be served. The more moderate length of dinners in
what are called " good houses " is a matter of general congratulation.
The six or four *entrées* have dwindled to two or three, and those
dreadful inventions known as sweets, rarely touched by man, have
also decreased, little savouries taking the place of the coloured
jellies and creams that formerly appeared in monotonous rotation.
By ten or half-past dinner is generally over. Coffee is brought into

the dining-room while the gentlemen smoke. Liquors and tea are offered during the evening, and keep up the flagging interest till the ladies ostensibly go to bed, after a little money has changed hands at poker or loo. Then the serious business of the night begins for the gentlemen, who dive into the recesses of the smoking-room. Brews of many kinds are prepared; effervescing waters, whisky, brandy, claret, lemons in profusion must be at hand. Many ladies at the present time, whose fortunes cannot be considered large, spend 600l. a year in their toilettes, and it is not unusual for 1,000l. to be spent on those who go out a great deal. Sixty guineas for a court dress is a not uncommon price. Entertainments are on a much more costly scale than formerly. Two thousand pounds are occasionally spent on flowers for one ball. The roses and lilies of the girls' complexions used to be considered the chief ornament of the room. Now, indeed, there are balls to which only three or four girls are invited—married women's balls, where the charms of the ladies can only be surpassed by the attractions of the supper.'

### Note 5.

Pleasure Boats.—The pleasure navy of England is a great fact, not to be ignored, as will be readily seen by a very brief sketch of some of the statistics connected with it. The number of yachts of all denominations on Hunt's List, which is the yachtsman's blue-book, for the year 1867, was 1,048. Their total tonnage was 59,876, the Northumbria, of 424 tons, owned by Mr. Stephenson, heading the list in point of size. Assuming one man to every 10 tons as the proper complement, we arrive at a figure just under 6,000 as the number of hands required to man them. Steam yachts, as a rule, require fewer hands than sailing yachts, cutters more than schooners, and, cæteris paribus, the proportion above assumed will be less in sailing yachts of large tonnage than those of small; but, after making all due allowances, one man to every 10 tons will be found to be a fair average. From the gross number, however, must be deducted a certain percentage in respect of those yachts which are laid up, which reduces the number of men afloat in any one year to 5,000. Taking the cost roughly, for the purpose of arriving at the total capital expended, say at 25l. per ton all round, we find it represented by a sum of 1,250,000l. These are large figures, and very suggestive of the growth of yachting up to the present time.—Once a Week.

The largest yacht now is the 'Amy,' of 812 tons register, owned by Mr. Stewart.

### Note 6.

A writer in the Contemporary Review on 'The Horse as an Instrument of Gambling' estimates the cost of race-horses as follows :—'The interest of the money sunk in racing stock is the least part of the cost which is incidental to keeping race-horses. It has been calculated—indeed, it is known from experience, and by

means of figures which cannot be doubted—that the annual expense
of keeping a race-horse is not less than 250*l*. per annum; indeed, it
has been set down by men well versed in the expenditure of the
turf at 300*l*., but we shall adopt the former figure.  In this amount
we include the trainers' and veterinary surgeons' accounts, all the
travelling and miscellaneous expenses incurred on behalf of the
animal, and a moderate allowance for entries to races.  That sum
(250*l*.) would, in the case of the many highly-bred youngsters, be
ridiculously insufficient, as such animals are entered, whilst still
yearlings, in a large number of races, the entry moneys to which
would more than absorb the whole of the sum we have named; but
when dealing with so many horses, an average of 250*l*. will just
about hit the mark, and it is better, if possible, to keep a little within
the expenditure than to overrate it.  Taking first the horses in
training, the annual cost of keeping these will amount, at 250*l*. each,
to 513,500*l*.  We shall not account in this estimate the keep of the
brood mares and sires, because horse-breeding, as a speculation, is
rewarded by the money obtained for the yearlings; and for the
board, lodging, and training of the seven hundred youngsters which
we have brought into this account, we shall allow for their first year
100*l*. for each, or a total sum for the year's expenses of 70,000*l*.,
which, added to the sum paid for the keep of the horses in training,
as explained above, will amount to a total of 583,500*l*. per annum,
to which, as representing the annual cost of our racing studs, must
be added the interest on the capital sunk in the business, so that
the yearly account will stand as follows :—Interest on capital expended on race-horses, 90,409*l*.; annual keep of horses, 583,500*l*.;
the total yearly expenditure being 673,950*l*.

### Note 7.

Writing on this subject M. Taine says:—

'My English friends confirm what I guessed about the large
number and the vastness of the private fortunes.  "Take a cab from
Sydenham; for five miles you will pass houses which indicate an
annual outlay of 1,500*l*. and upwards."  According to the official
statistics of 1841, there are one million of servants to every sixteen
millions of inhabitants.  The liberal professions are much better
remunerated than on the Continent.  I know a musician at Leipzig
of first-class talent; he receives 3*s*. a lesson at the Academy of
Leipzig, 6*s*. in the city, and one guinea in London.  The visit of a
doctor, who is not celebrated, costs 4*s*. or 9*s*. in Paris, and a guinea
here.  With us a professor at the College of France receives 300*l*.,
at the Sorbonne, 480*l*., at the School of Medicine, 400*l*.  A professor
at Oxford, a head of a house, has often from 1,000*l*. to 3,000*l*.  Tenny-
son, who writes little, is said to make 5,000*l*. a year.  The head-master
at Eton has a salary of 6,080*l*.; of Harrow, 6,280*l*.; of Rugby, 2,960*l*.
Many of the masters in these establishments have salaries from 1,200*l*.
to 1,240*l*.—one of them at Harrow has 2,220*l*.  The Bishop of London

has 10,000*l.* a year; the Archbishop of York has 15,000*l.* An article is paid for at the rate of 8*l.* the sheet in the *Revue des Deux Mondes*, and 20*l.* in the English *Quarterlies.* The *Times* has paid a 100*l.* for a certain article. Thackeray, the novelist, has made 160*l.* in twenty-four hours through the medium of two lectures, the one being delivered in Brighton, the other in London. From the magazine to which he contributed his novels he received 2,000*l.* a year, and 10*l.* a page in addition; this magazine had 100,000 subscribers. He estimated his own yearly earnings at 4,800*l.* It must be understood that I put on one side the enormous fortunes made in manufactures, those of the nobility, the profits or revenues of 200,000*l.* yearly; their outlay is proportionate. A young engineer, a younger son, who was obliged to make his fortune, said to me, " With 8,000*l.* yearly one is not wealthy in England; one is merely very comfortably off.'' Another, who spends his summers in the country, added, "Look at the family circles of our farms; their daughters learn to play on the piano ; they dress splendidly.'' The rule is to make much and spend much. An Englishman does not put anything aside, does not think of the future—at the most he insures his life; in this he is the reverse of a Frenchman, who is saving and abstemious.'

## *Note* 8.

The following is an account of ' A Collier's Play Day in Lancashire ' during a period of big wages, taken from the *Manchester Examiner* :—' Inquiries on a dry and somewhat heating subject pursued in the neighbourhood of Ince led our representative on a Monday afternoon, about a fortnight ago, into one of the many beerhouses which the village contains, and there, alone with a modest refreshment of the inner man, he obtained the information, added gratis, that a big " wrestle '' was to take place that afternoon between a Wigan man and a rival from Spring Green for 20*l.* a side. A mild expression of interest in a local event of so much importance was met with an almost fierce offer to back the Wigan man for a sovereign. Shortly afterwards, meeting an extensive colliery proprietor in the neighbourhood, to whom we imparted the valuable information obtained in the public-house, we were amused and instructed by the peculiar nature of the evident interest which he took in the intelligence. He trusted that the Wigan man might be worsted, and this on the basely selfish ground that, as his own colliers would certainly stake their money upon the local favourite and lose their bets, they would the sooner return to their work in the mine ; but if their pockets were lined by winnings from Spring Green, their return to work would be proportionately delayed, and so many more pounds would be lost to himself. The entrance to the recreation ground was thronged, and lads were pouring in rapidly on a payment of 6*d.* per head. It turned out, however, that the wrestling which had been announced as the *pièce de résistance* of the afternoon's entertainment was not the first article on the programme. In a far part of the field another competition was about to commence. The roof of a tumbledown shanty, known as 'the grand stand,' overlooking a dusty road, was crowded with youths (each nursing under his arm a faithful dog, swaddled in cosy housings) who had paid a small extra fee for admission to this point of vantage. Within the stand a rough-and-ready refreshment stall, whereat spirits were sold in appetising "nips," was doing a brisk business. The noble sportsmen ensconced on the roof of the stand, as well as the plebeian crowd below, were eagerly arguing and betting as to the respective merits of two jumpers, who were about to test their powers against each other for 10*l.* a side. By-and-by one of the competitors, familiarly known as "Adam," who appeared to be the favourite, strode out from a small dressing-room nominally partitioned off from the refreshment bar by a strip of paling. He appeared conspicuous among the admirers who surrounded him by the oddity of his costume, which was confined to a woollen shirt at least as short as that which gave her name to Tam O'Shanter's weird *innamorata*, and a pair of clogs! Here was the ludicrous story of the King of Ashantee, whose court dress was a cocked hat and a walking-stick, reproduced before our eyes in Christian England —at least, at Wigan. The apparition was startling enough to modest youth, but hey, presto, change! and our marvelling eyes are entertained with a study of the nude. The shirt is doffed, and, saving the clogs aforesaid and the slightest possible cincture round the hips, the shivering miner stood before his rapt admirers in *puris naturalibus*—excepting, indeed, that his skin was a trifle dirty. By-and-by the rival jumper, a younger and shorter man, strutted forth, and the two champions marched up and down in front of the refreshment booth, the Hebes there attendant joining unabashed in the circle of critical and appreciative admirers of this free and open display of the human form divine. It is no part of our intention to describe the animated contest which ensued. Betting was very free, chiefly for small sums, and in this part of the sport the younger lads were particularly conspicuous. The interest manifested in the match was at times so irrepressible that a clear jumping space could with difficulty be maintained, and the managers of the ground could only maintain order by occasional threats to interrupt the match. The betting continued brisk throughout these disturbances, and was maintained even after the match was closed. When the result was ascertained and declared, pigeons were liberated by many of the onlookers, and went whirling off to distant villages, bearing information as to the winner. A second match, for 5*l.* a side, followed under precisely similar circumstances, in the presence of a crowd which momentarily became more unruly.

'When the jumping match was concluded the field was cleared out, and then we became aware that to be witnesses of the wrestling we must pay an extra sixpence for readmission. Two or three professional bettors had stands erected on the confines of the crowd and did a brisk trade. The athletes stripped in full view of the sightseers. The match resulted again in favour of the Wigan favourite in the first two bouts, and the sport, though exciting enough while it lasted, was soon over. Attention was once or twice distracted from it by the quarrels of drunken men on the outskirts of the crowd. The day's amusement was finally closed by a tragedy which was thus recorded in the newspapers of the Wednesday following :—

'*Fatal Termination of a Wrestling Match.*—At the conclusion of a prize wrestling match at Ince Recreation Grounds, near Wigan, on Monday, two men, natives of Ince, were forced by their companions into a similar contest. · Stakes of some amount were posted, and the men, who were in a state of semi-drunkenness at the time, on meeting, indulged in some unprofessional play, and at length all laws relating to the sport were entirely disregarded, and the brutal performance terminated by one of the wrestlers, named Henry Crowthers, receiving a fall which broke his neck, and ended his existence at ten o'clock yesterday morning. The coroner's jury found from the evidence that the wrestling bout had been carried on within the laws of the game, but censured the friends of the parties for allowing a drunken man to engage in such a contest. This unhappy accident has attracted attention to the Ince Recreation Grounds, and a movement inimical to their continued existence is being vigorously prosecuted by the vicar of the parish. A fear that the sporting miner might again find his way to Newton Heath in the event of their disestablishment is the only motive which could induce us to offer a syllable against the worthy clergyman's laudable endeavour.'

The following is a typical newspaper notice :—' "*Big Pay-Day* " at *Greenock.*—Greenock was in a state of unusual uproar on Saturday afternoon and night in consequence of its being a " big pay-day." There were frequent riots, which were with difficulty suppressed by the police, who in several instances suffered severely. Upwards of fifty of the rioters were arrested.'

*Note 9.*

Of the fact of the increase, especially in local taxation, there is no doubt. At the same time it will probably be found that relatively to the population and the wealth of the country the burden of taxation is now far lighter than in previous periods ; and that in this respect we are in a more favourable position than that of the foreign countries who compete with us in the markets of the world.—*Report of Commissioners on Depression of Trade*, Clause 85.

*Note 10,*

The Rev. Charles Joseph, in his evidence before the Artisan's Dwelling Inquiry Committee, in the Borough of Birmingham, in

June last, gave some interesting facts on the relation of wages to
house rent in Birmingham, respecting twenty families—father,
mother, and an average of 3·5 children each.   Their average wages
amounted to 27s. 6d. weekly (exclusive of all other sources of income), and they paid on an average 6s. a week of rent, or in the
proportion of 23·7 per cent., but the proportion varied from 15·6 to
33·3 per cent. of the wages.   It appears, moreover, that sober men
paid 40 per cent. more rent, and were in that degree better housed
than drunken men, the average of the sober man giving 33s. 4d.
wages and 5s. rent, and of drunken men 31s. 8d. wages and 3s. rent.
And these facts respecting house rent may be taken to represent the
case of most of our large towns.—LEVI'S *Wages and Earnings of
the Working Classes*, p. 31.

### Note 11.

Mr. William Hoyle, whom I had the pleasure of knowing, was
the great authority on drink statistics, and devoted much of his
time to the investigation of the subject.

His works on ' Our National Resources, and How they are Wasted,'
and ' Our National Drink Bill,' are well worthy of attention.

From his last letter to the *Times* the following remarks are
quoted :—

'A sovereign wasted by dissipation injures trade as much as
one wasted by idleness or by bad management in producing ; nay,
often more, for if the wasting process, as too often happens, is accompanied by burdens and evils, then, by the extent of the evils so
produced, will the mischief resulting in the latter case exceed that
of the former.

' It is not so much the fixed wealth of a nation that creates demand for goods as its current income.   The former is applied
mostly to producing, and the latter to purchasing ; and inasmuch as
the current income is the purchasing fund from which must come
the nation's demand for commodities, it will be evident that all
waste of the same, by lessening the purchasing fund of the nation,
must decrease the demand for commodities, and so make it more
difficult for manufacturers to keep their works going ; here lies the
explanation of the long continuance and severity of the present depression in trade.

' It is a question of waste of income, and if the prodigality of some
were not compensated for by the thrift and industry of others, the
nation would soon not only have a depressed but a bankrupt trade.

' In one of its trenchant leaders the *Times* a short while ago remarked :—

' " Drinking baffles us, confounds us, shames us, and mocks us at
every point.   It outwits alike the teacher, the man of business, the
patriot, and the legislator.

' " Every other institution flounders in hopeless difficulties ; the
public-house hold its triumphant course."

'The signs of the times presage that the day is drawing near when this great nation will refuse its consent to the existence of a traffic that "outwits," "baffles," "confounds," and "mocks" it in all its efforts for the good of the nation, and which is so mischievous and demoralising as to cause the institutions which are established for the people's welfare "to flounder in hopeless difficulties."—I remain, yours very truly,

WILLIAM HOYLE.'

# APPENDIX TO 'PROGRESS.'

## Note 1.

It is, however, right to point out that, while the share of the aggregate wealth produced in the country which now falls to labour is larger than it was twenty years ago, a corresponding diminution has taken place in the share which falls to capital ; in other words that while wages have risen, profits have fallen ; and that this is obviously a process which cannot be continued beyond a certain point. This point has, we think, been very nearly, if not quite, attained already.

A time may therefore come when capital will lose all inducement to lend itself to the work of production, and if the employer is driven out of the field, the labourer will necessarily suffer with him.—*Report of Commissioners on Depression of Trade*, Clause 83.

## Note 2.

From the Reports of the Commissioners of Inland Revenue, it appears that between the years 1874-5 and 1884-5 the number of incomes assessed under Schedule D, amounting to 200*l*. a year and upwards, increased from 184,354 to 239,367, being an increase of nearly 30 per cent.

But it is to be observed that the number increased at a much more rapid rate at the lower end of the scale than at the upper, as the following table, compiled from the Reports, will show :—

SCHEDULE D. TRADES AND PROFESSIONS ONLY. NUMBER OF PERSONS ASSESSED IN THE YEARS 1874-75, 1879-80, AND 1884-85 IN THE UNDERMENTIONED CLASSES :—

| Incomes from | 1874-75 | 1879-80 | 1884-85 | Increase 1884-85 over 1874-75 | Rate per cent. of increase |
|---|---|---|---|---|---|
| £ £ | No. | No. | No. | No. | |
| 200 to 1,000 | 162,435 | 197,775 | 215,790 | 53,355 | 32·85 |
| 1,000 „ 2,000 | 11,944 | 12,011 | 13,403 | 1,459 | 12·21 |
| 2,000 „ 3,000 | 3,797 | 3,604 | 4,038 | 241 | 6·34 |
| 3,000 „ 4,000 | 1,857 | 1,664 | 1,914 | 57 | 3·07 |
| 4,000 „ 5,000 | 1,003 | 898 | 1,074 | 71 | 7·07 |
| 5,000 „ 10,000 | 2,035 | 1,671 | 1,928 | [1]107 | [1]5·25 |
| 10,000 and upwards | 1,283 | 1,020 | 1,220 | [1]63 | [1]4·91 |
| Total . . . | 184,354 | 218,643 | 239,367 | 55,013 | 29·84 |

[1] Decrease.

From this table it would appear that the number of persons with incomes of less than 2,000*l.* a year has increased at a more rapid rate than the population (which in the period in question increased about 10 per cent.), while the number of persons with incomes above 2,000*l.* has increased at a less rapid rate, and the number with incomes above 5,000*l.* has actually diminished ; and further, that the lower the income the more rapid the rate of increase.

We think, therefore, that, whether the aggregate amount of profits is increasing or not, there is distinct evidence that profits are becoming more widely distributed among the classes engaged in trade and industry; and that, while the larger capitalists may be receiving a lower return than that to which they have been accustomed, the number of those who are making a profit, though possibly a small one, has largely increased.—*Report of Commissioners on Depression of Trade*, p. xvi.

*Note 3.*

In 1870 the total number of adult able-bodied paupers in England and Wales was 194,089 ; in 1880 it had fallen to 126,000 ; and in 1884 it had further decreased to 98,071.—JEANS' *England's Supremacy*, p. 282.

*Note 4.*

There is no reliable evidence of the physique of the people at any distinct period. The Anthropometric Committee of the British Association[1] recently made extensive observations respecting the height, weight, girth of chest, drawing power, and other particulars of the people in different parts of the country, which will afford a useful standard whereby to compare their future progress. But no such observations were made before, and loose opinions that the people are apparently smaller or taller now than they were are not reliable data to go by.

The general results of the inquiry relating to adult persons of the ages from 23 to 50 years were as follows :—

| — | Average height, statute inches, without shoes | Average weight, including clothes | Ratio lbs. weight per inch of statute height |
|---|---|---|---|
| | | lbs. | |
| England . . . . | 67·36 | 155·0 | 2·301 |
| Wales . . . . . | 66·66 | 158·3 | 2·375 |
| Scotland . . . . | 68·71 | 165·3 | 2·406 |
| Ireland . . . . | 67·90 | 154·1 | 2·270 |

LEVI'S *Wages and Earnings of the Working Classes*, pp. 25-26.

[1] See *Transactions of the British Association for the Advancement of Science*, 1882.

PRINTED BY
SPOTTISWOODE AND CO., NEW-STREET SQUARE
LONDON

*10*